Mellowing MANDALAS #3
ADULT COLORING BOOK

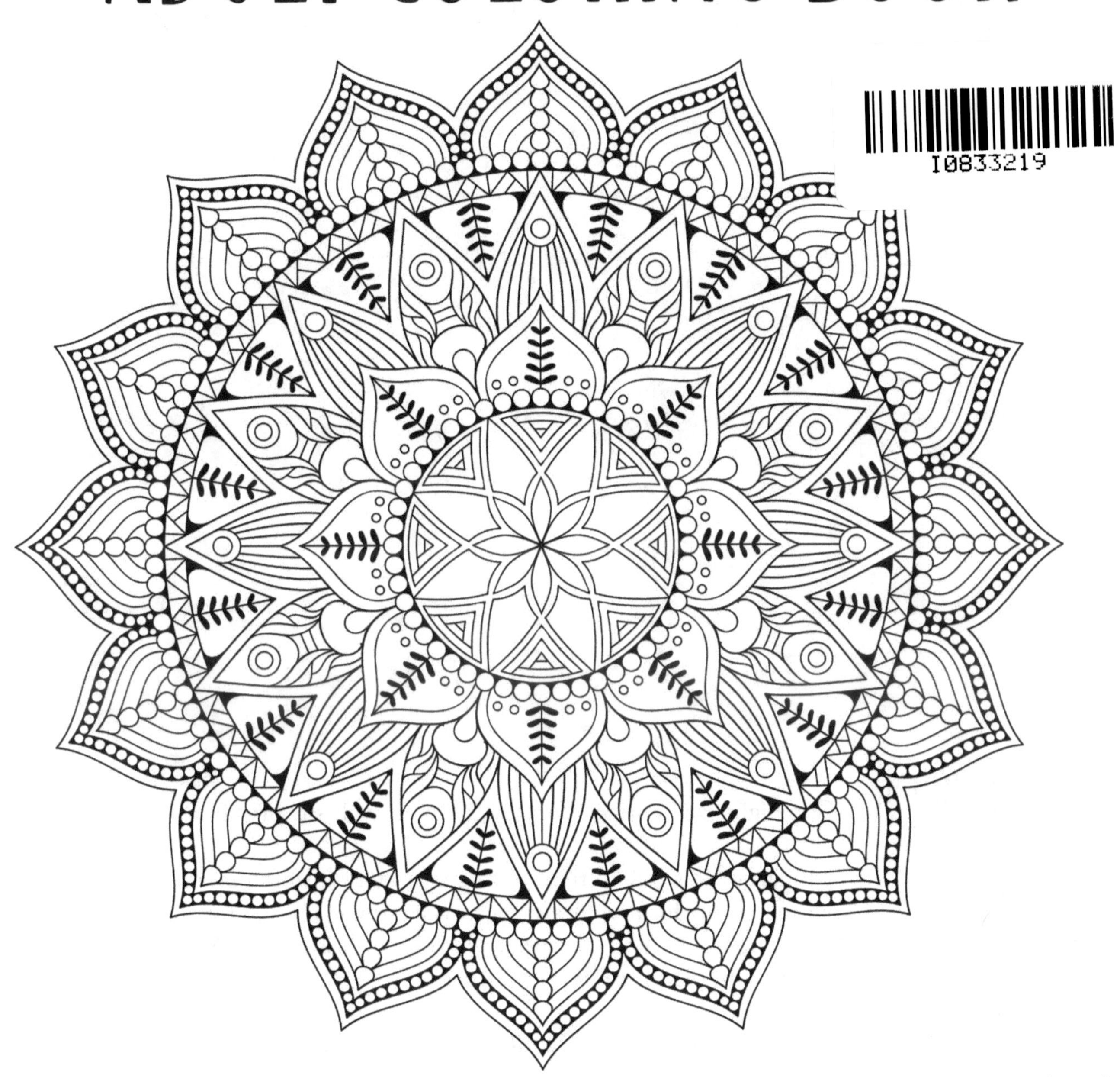

I0833219

42 All-New, Custom-drawn Mandala Designs for Your Coloring Delight

COLORING WITH JOY PUBLISHING

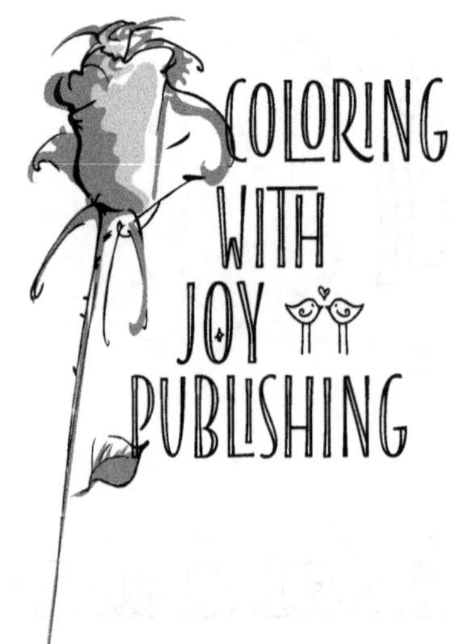

Copyright, ©Coloring With Joy, 2016, all rights reserved.

No part of this publication may be reproduced, stored in a retrieval system, or transmitted, in any form or by any means, electronic, mechanical, photocopying, recording, or otherwise, without the prior written permission of the author. To receive written permission, please see the back matter.

Book and Cover Design: Joy Rose
Mandala Cover Design, *Sid Ork,* for Coloring With Joy Publishing

ISBN: 978-0-9978133-4-0
Published and created in the United States of America
Printed in the United States of America

Title Page image available for coloring on page 71.

To my coloring friends:

Are you ready for some more color? Welcome to **Book #3** in our popular Mellowing Mandalas series. We all know that a little doodling and coloring goes a long way toward reducing stress. We're delighted to bring you our third new adult coloring book for your fun and relaxation. We've included a great mix of brand-new, custom-drawn mandalas in this collection of **42 designs on more than 90 pages.**

As usualy, some of the designs are quite complex and others are very simple. We know what it's like. One day, you want to tackle something detailed, and on another, you just want to doodle a bit, with a cuppa coffee or tea. Our variety gives you *wonderful* choices, allowing you to pick what you want based on your mood or just how much time you have to yourself. For the kids, we've even included one or two for the younger members of your household, to keep them busy while you're relaxing with more compex creations. Some of the designs are *fierce* and some are whimsical.

Page numbers are displayed in a light grey, on the back of each drawing page, only. To make it easy for you to find where you left off.

Each image is backed with a blank page. Two extra blank pages are included at the back, for you to cut out and place between your book pages while you are coloring, to protect against any bleed-through.

We love to hear feedback and suggestions. Please see page 89 to find our Contact email address. Don't hesitate to write me!

We hope that you'll love this third book in the series, and that you'll have fun and relax when *Coloring With Joy.*

Have a blast!

JOY ROSE

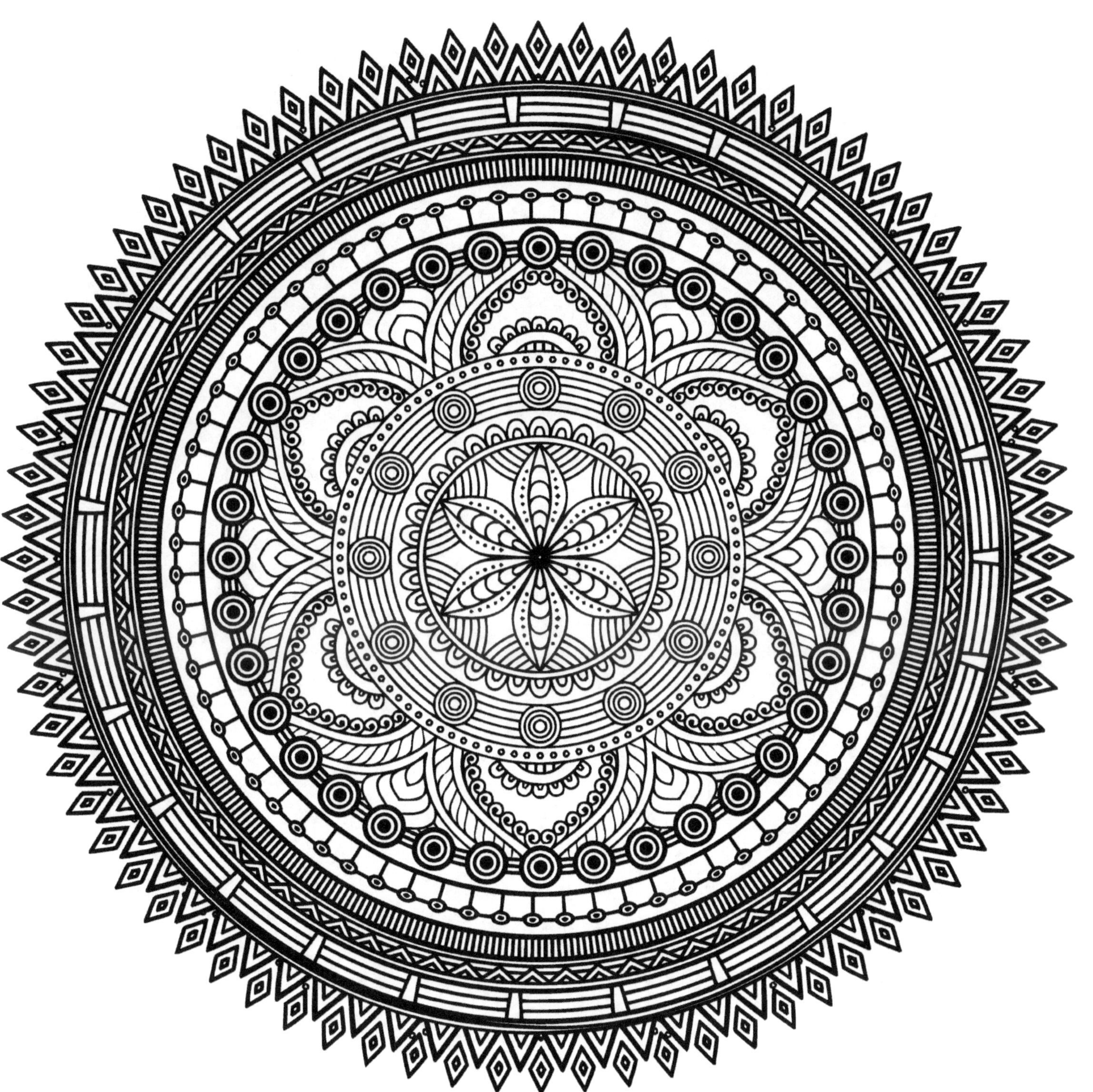

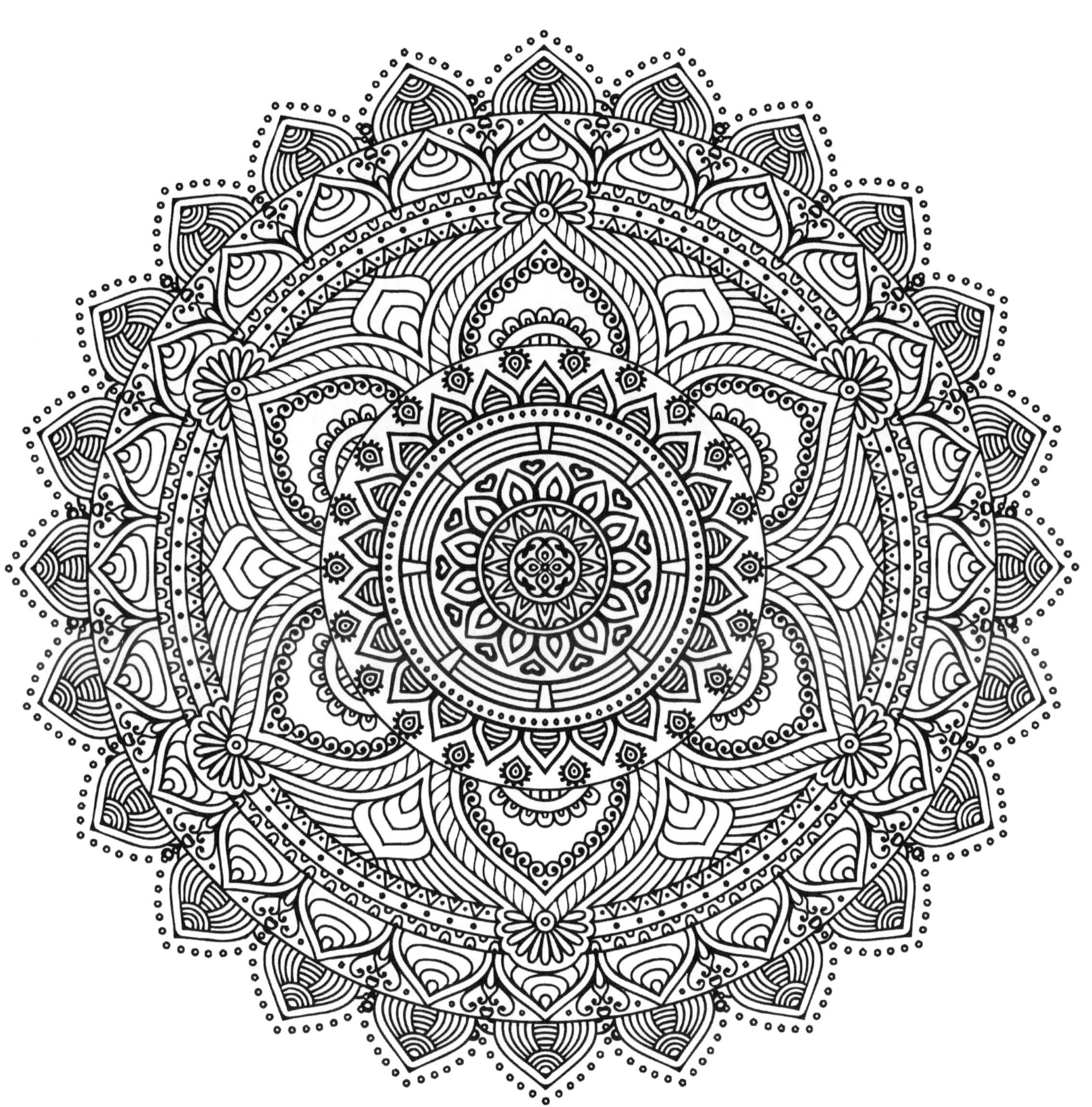

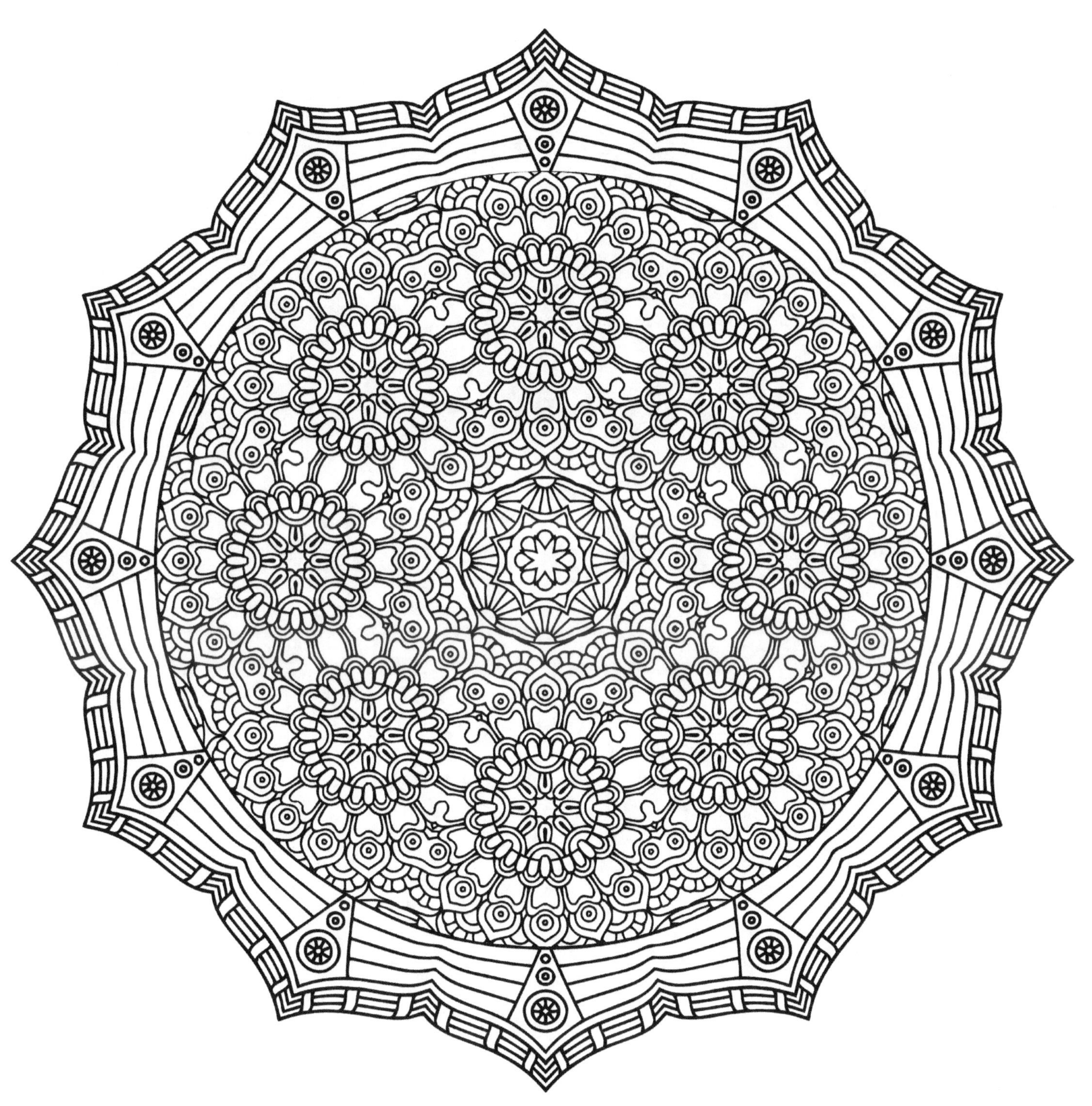

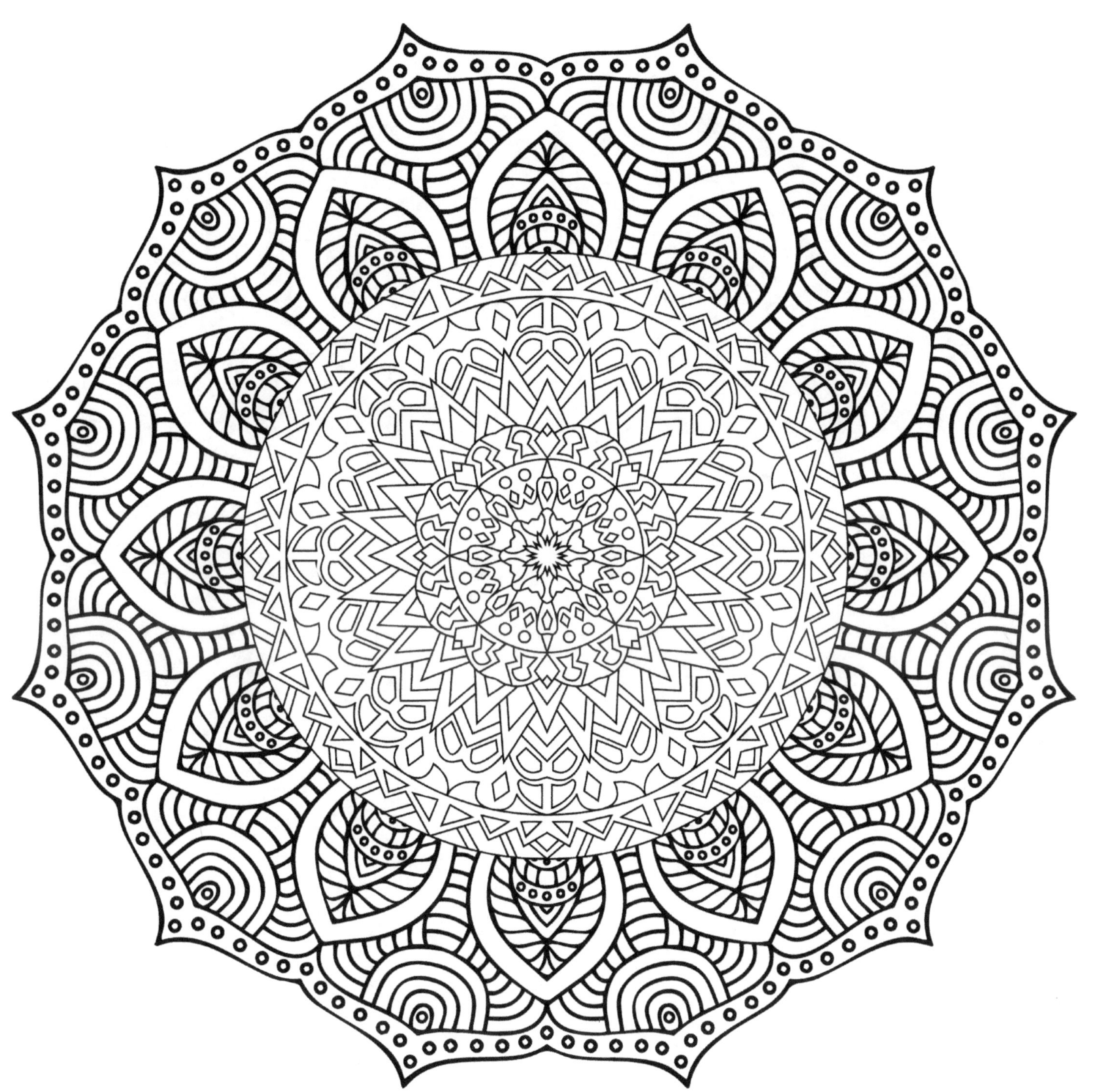

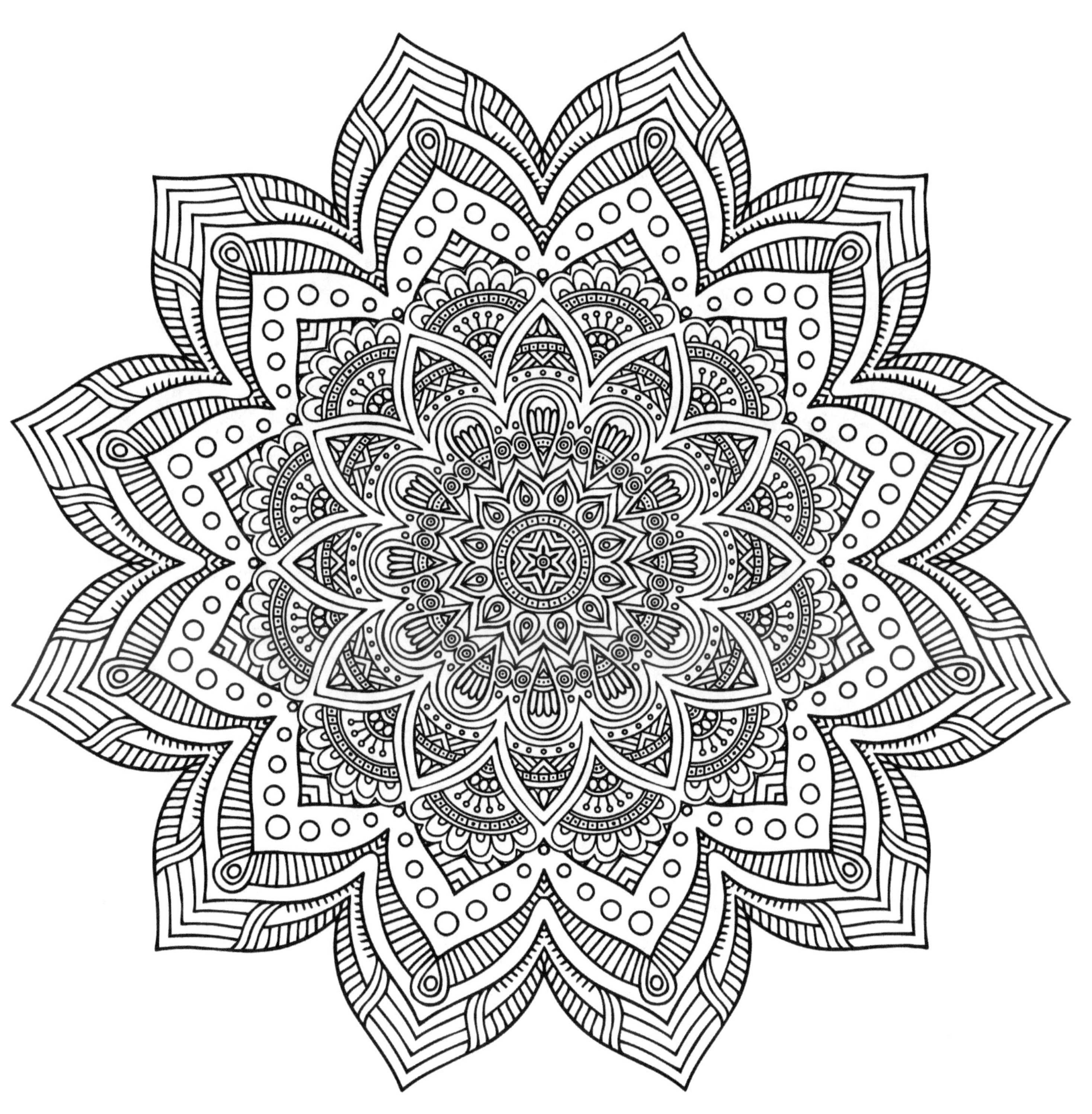

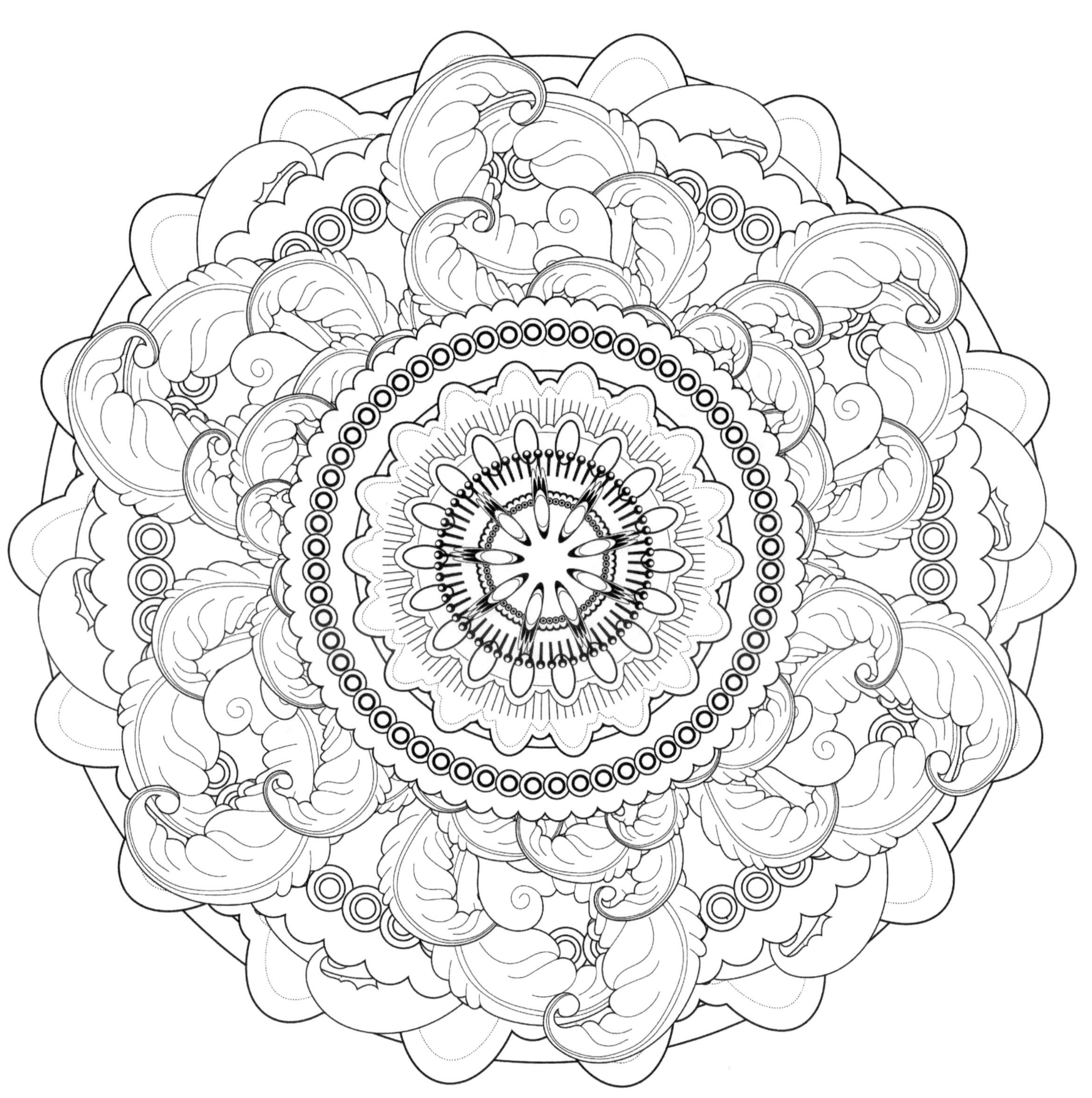

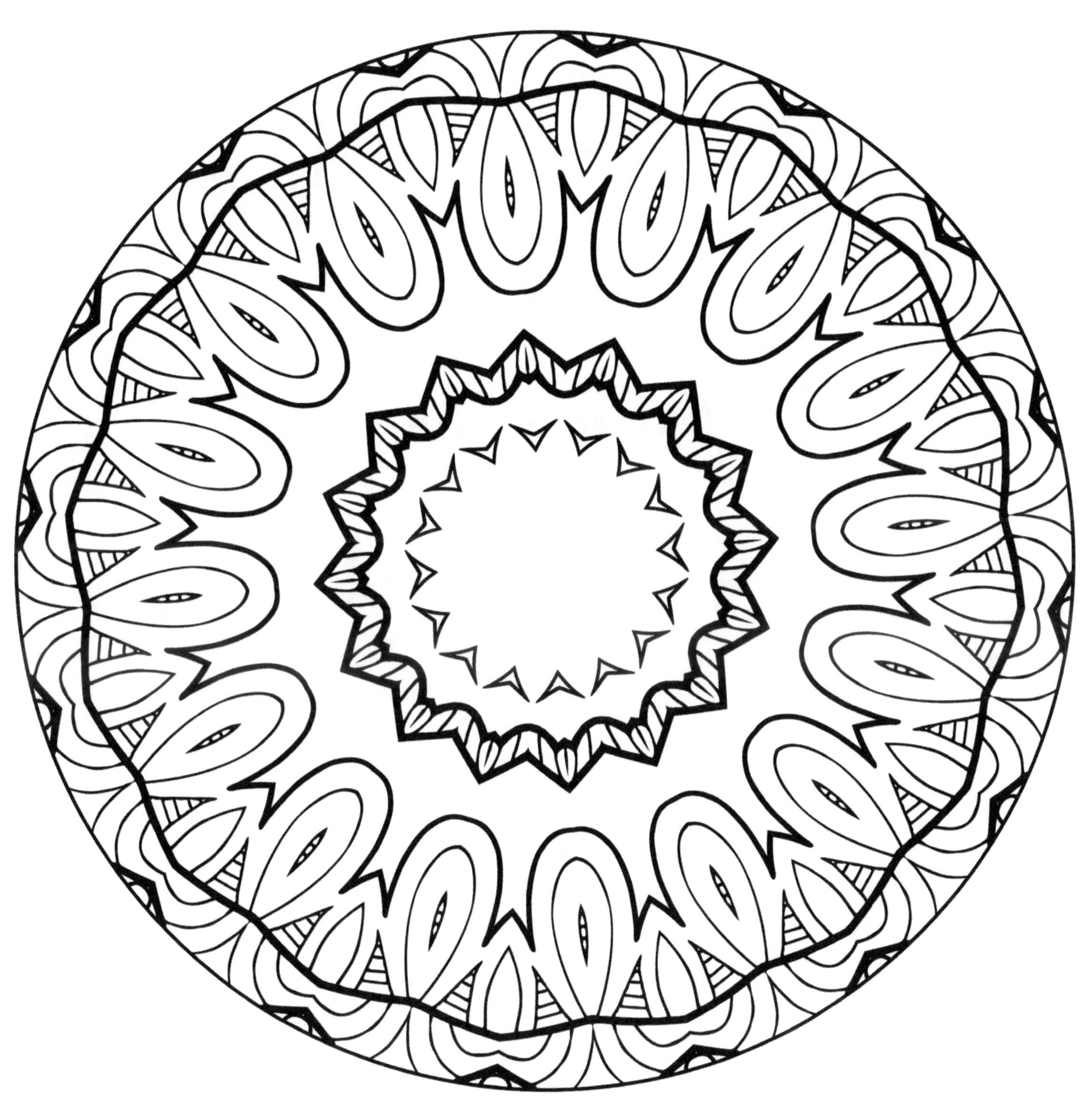

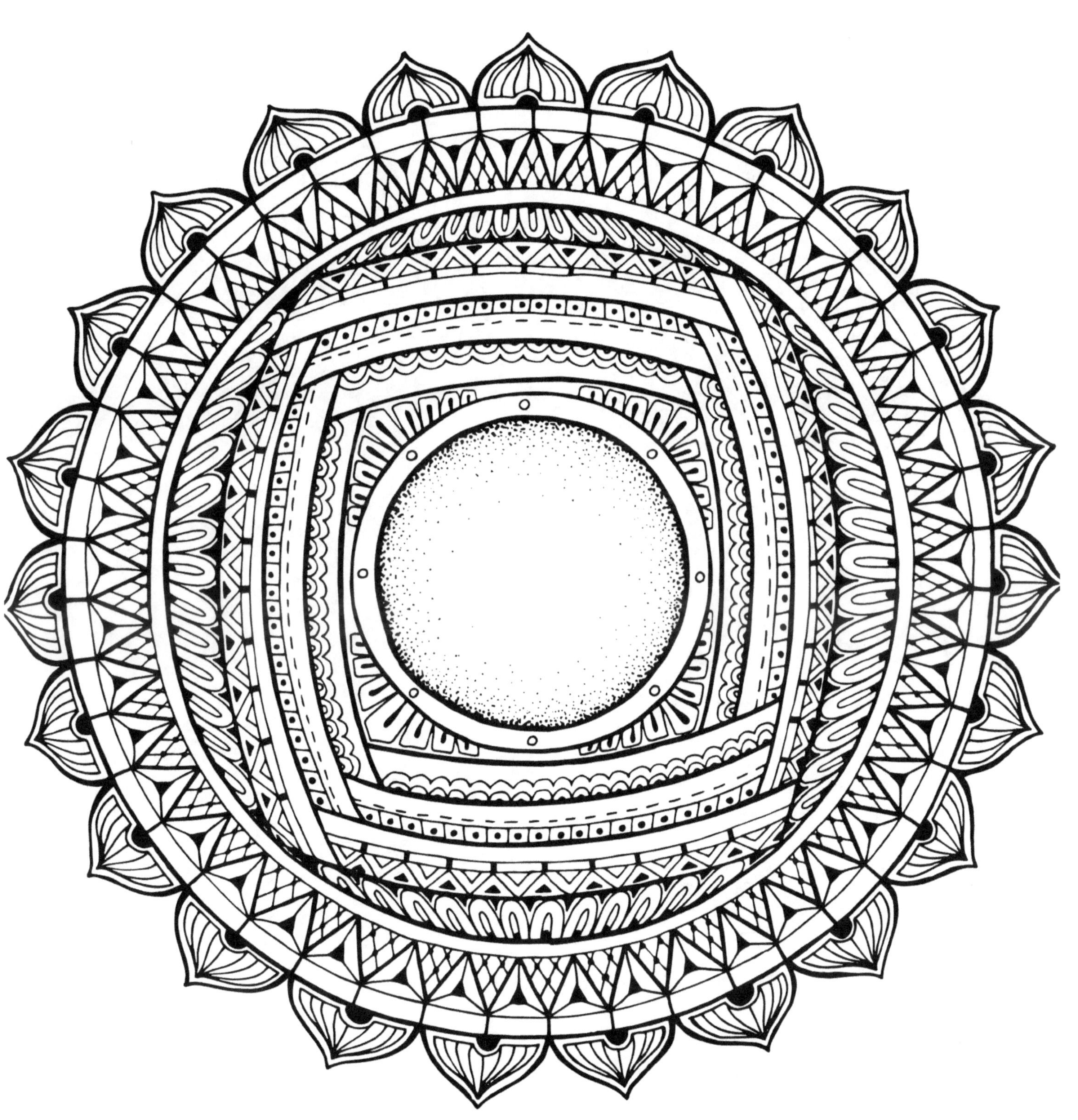

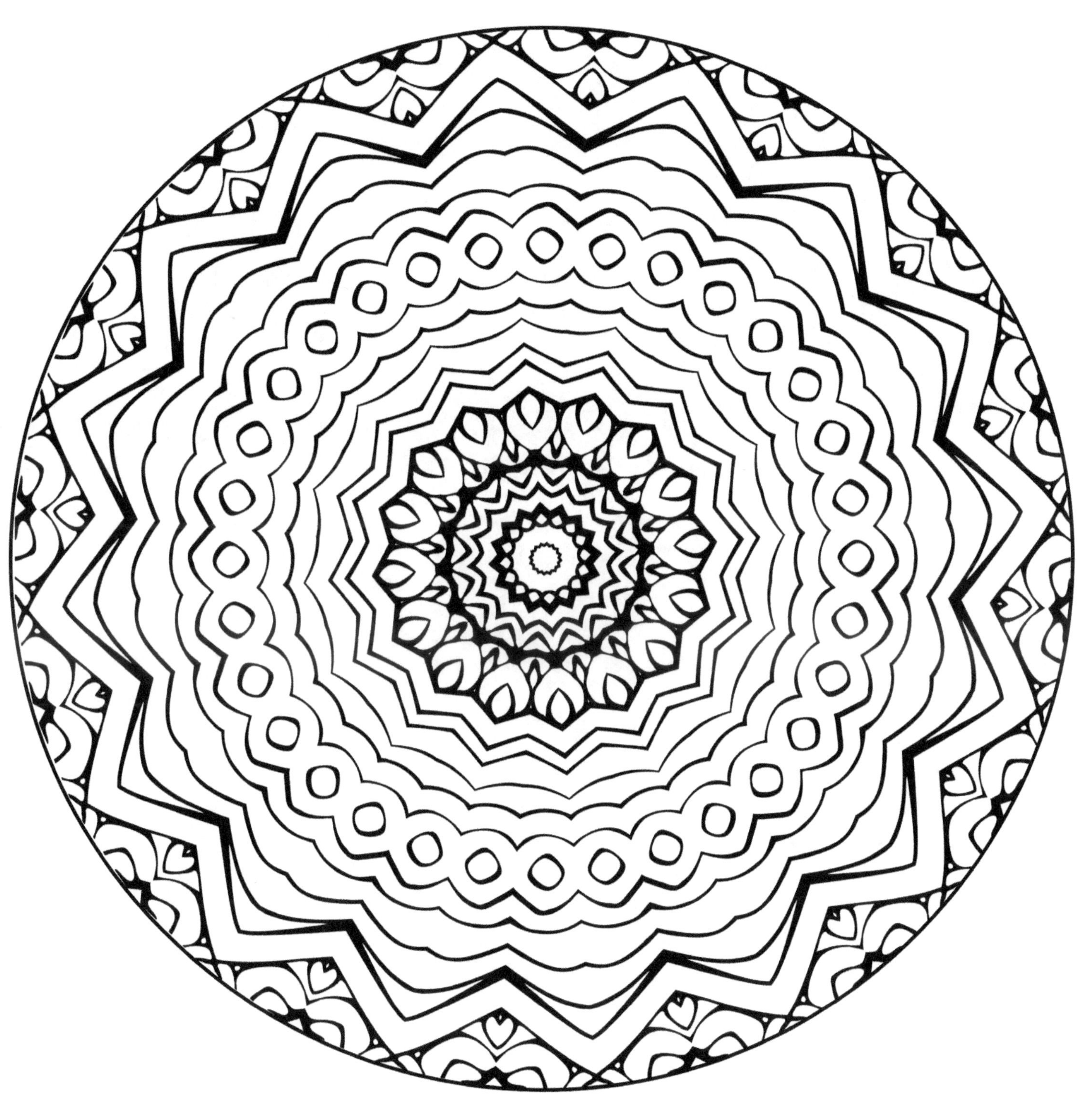

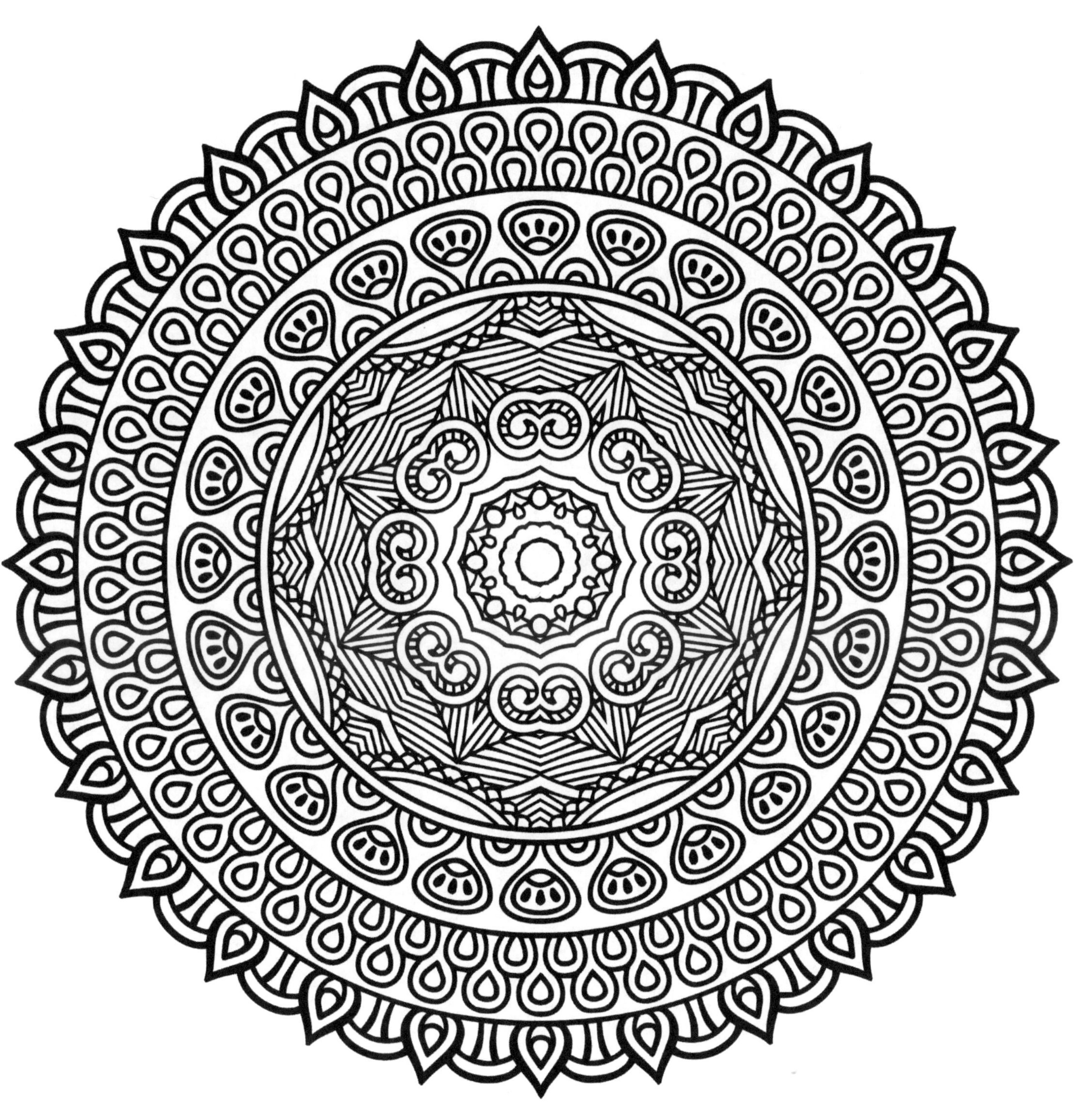

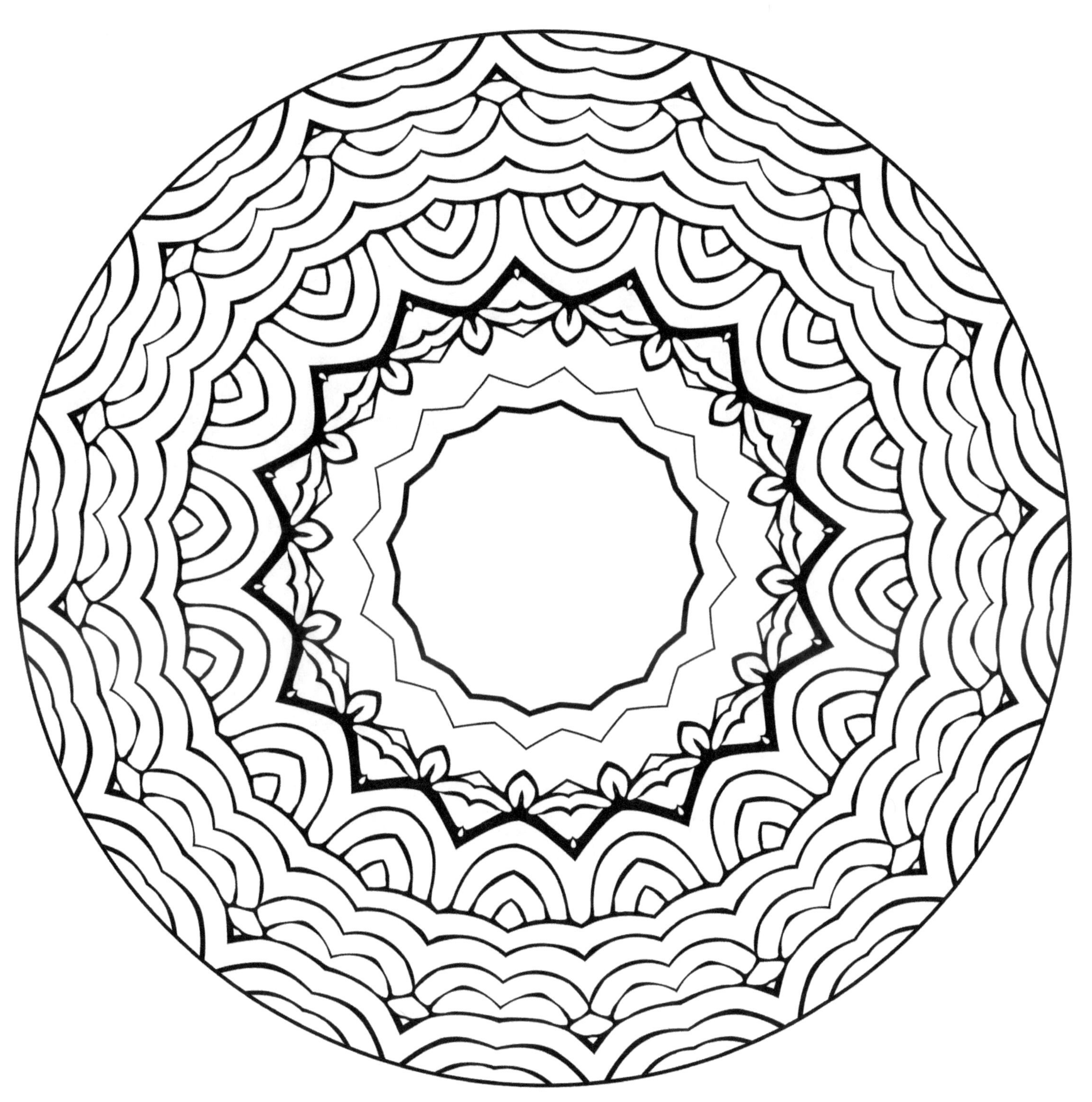

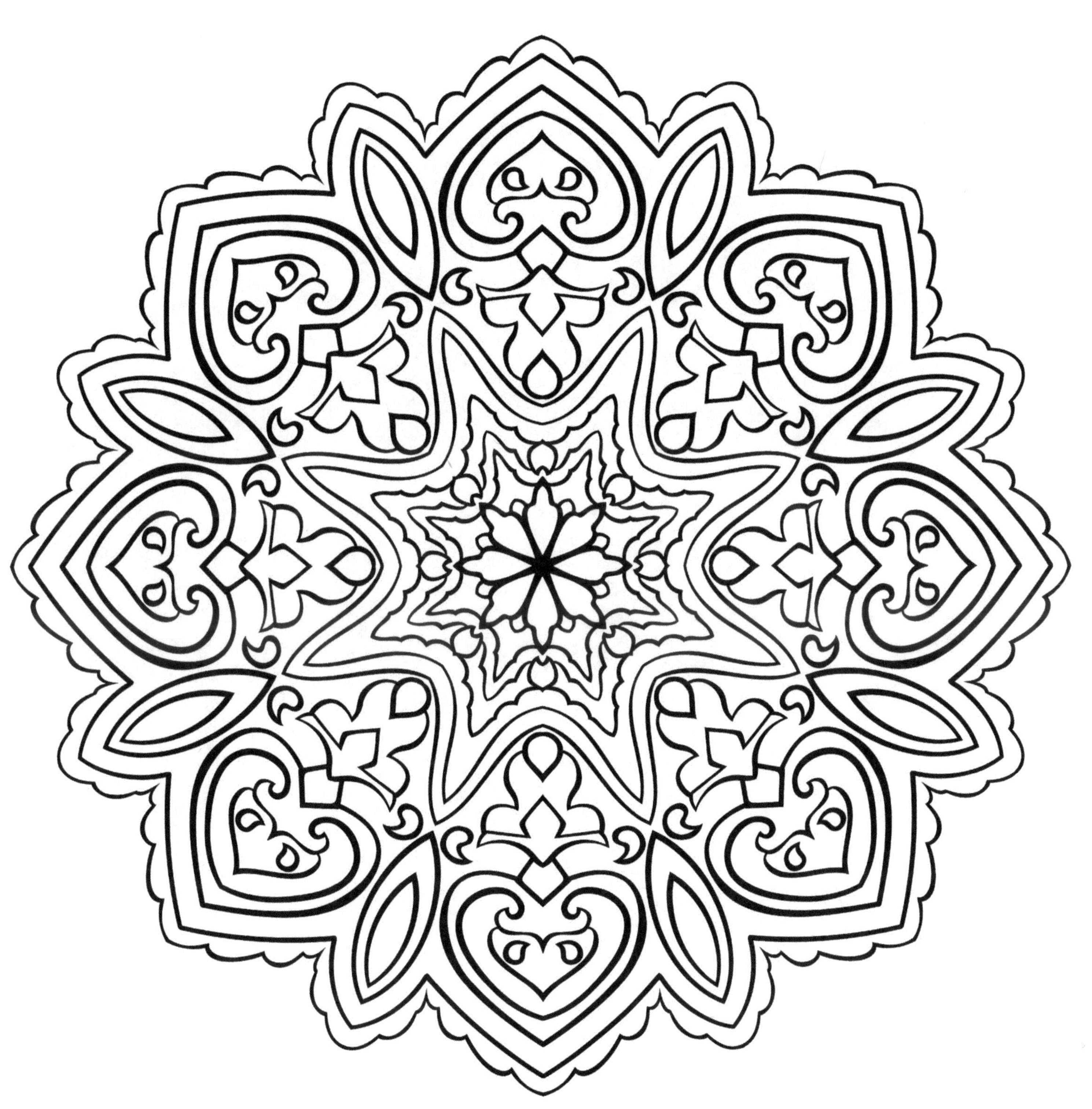

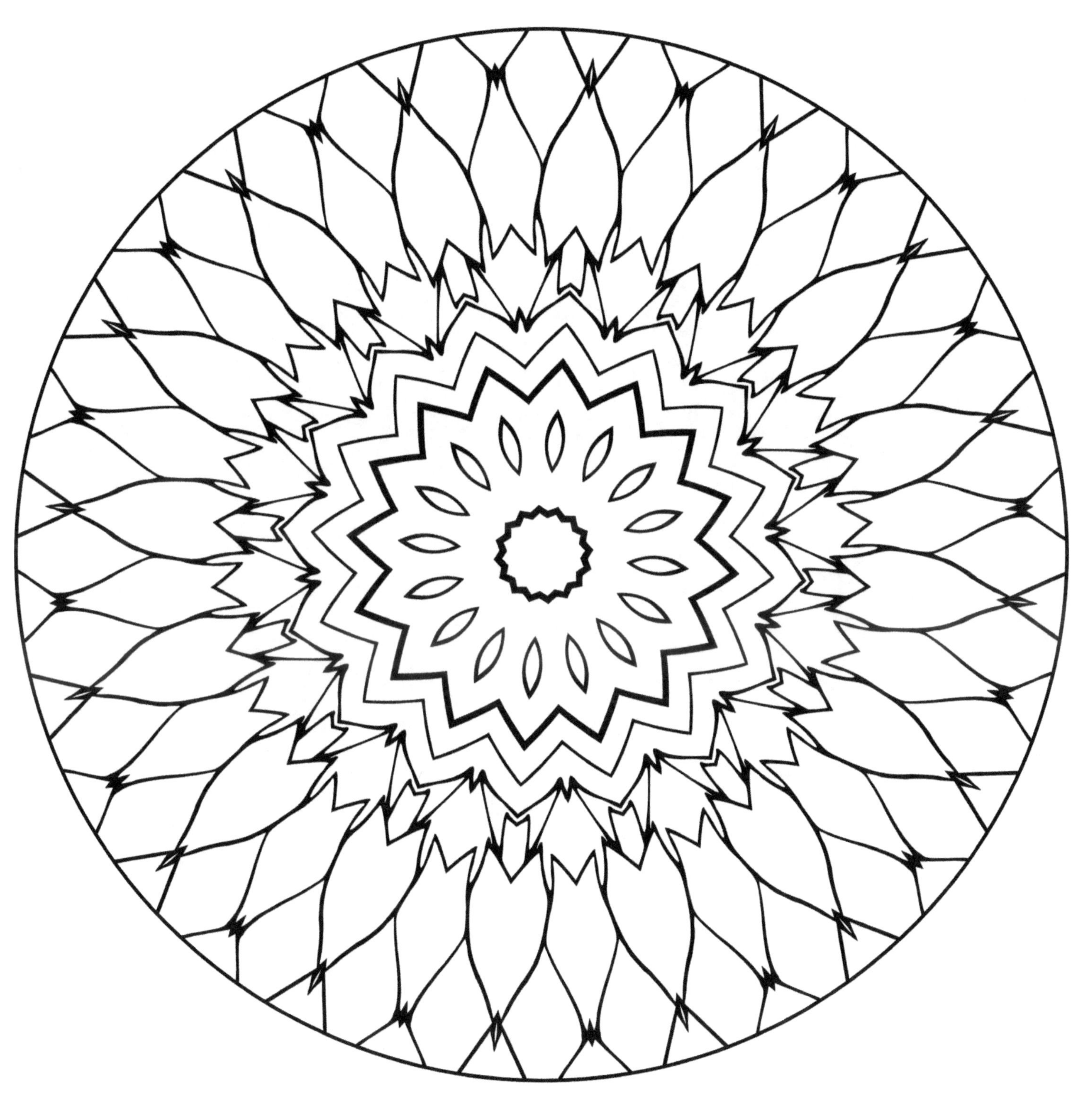

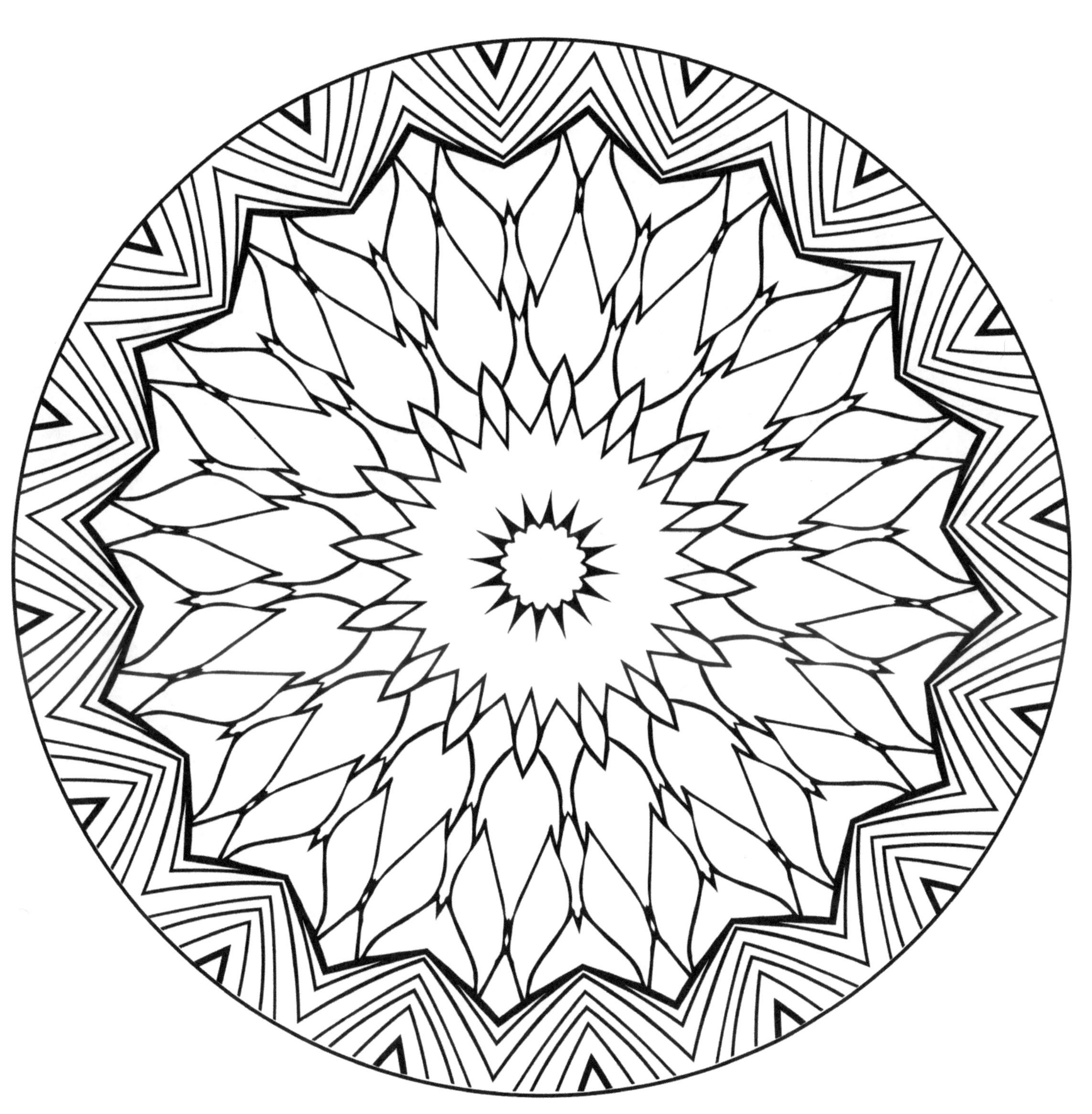

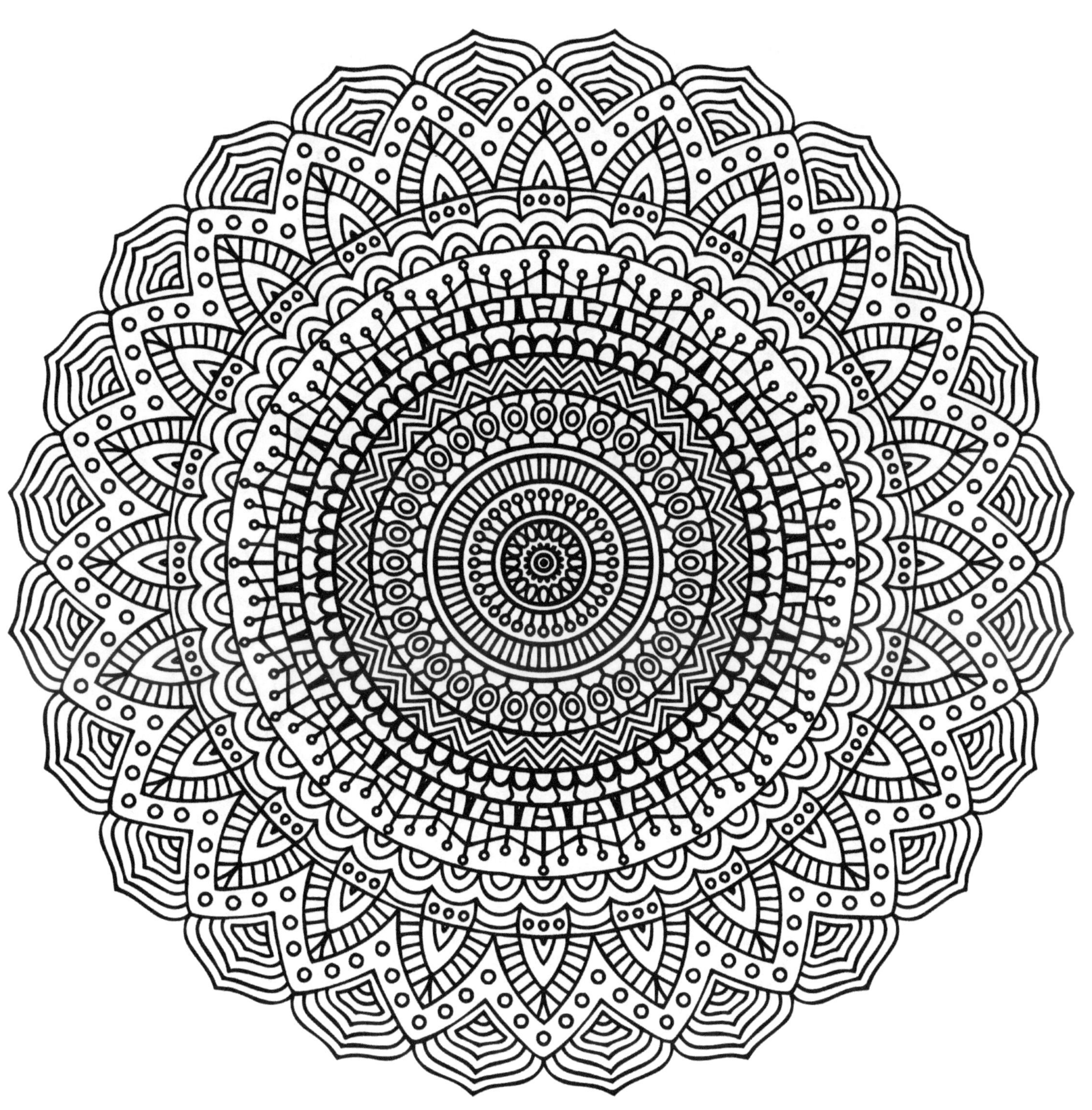

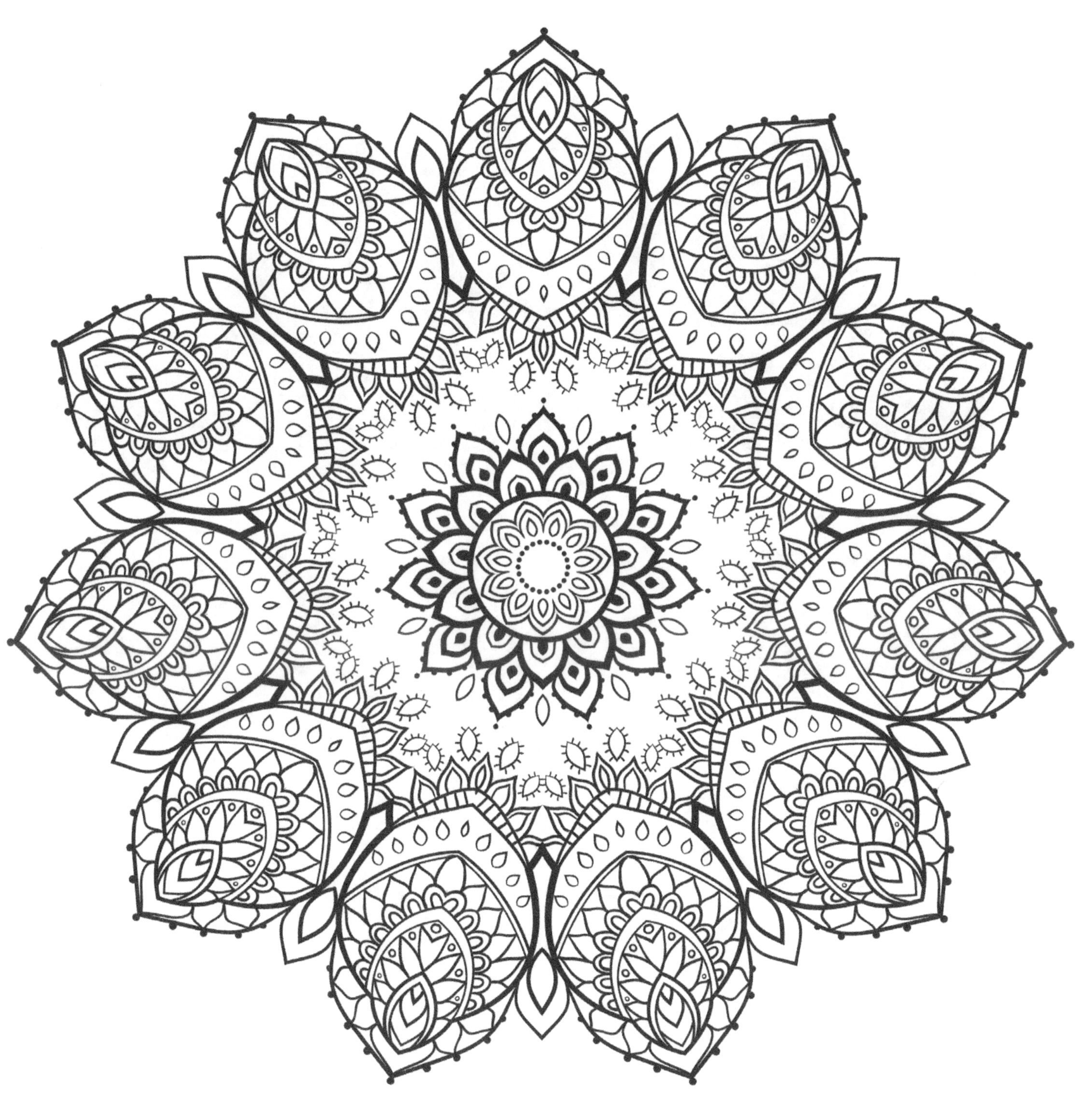

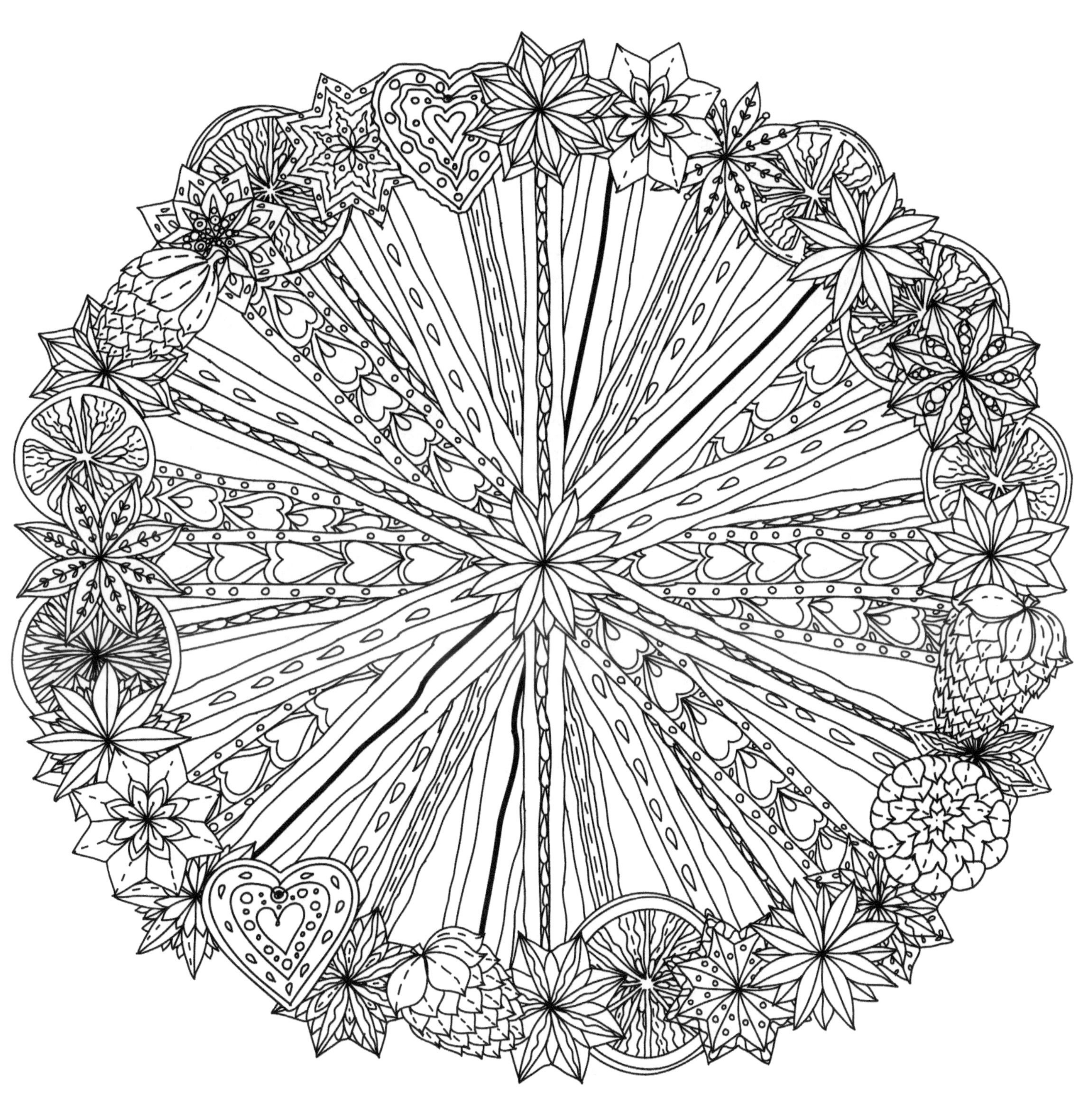

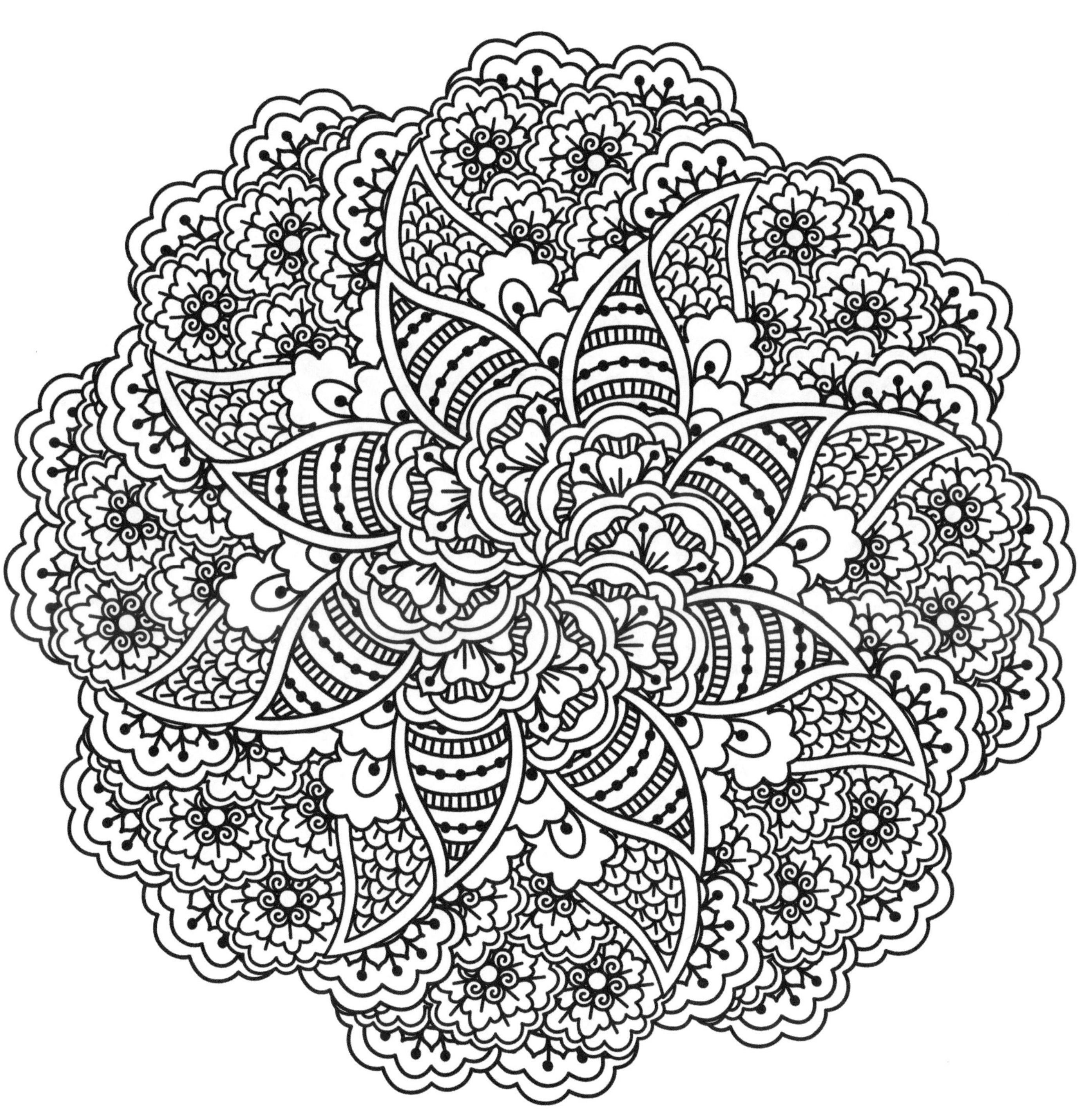

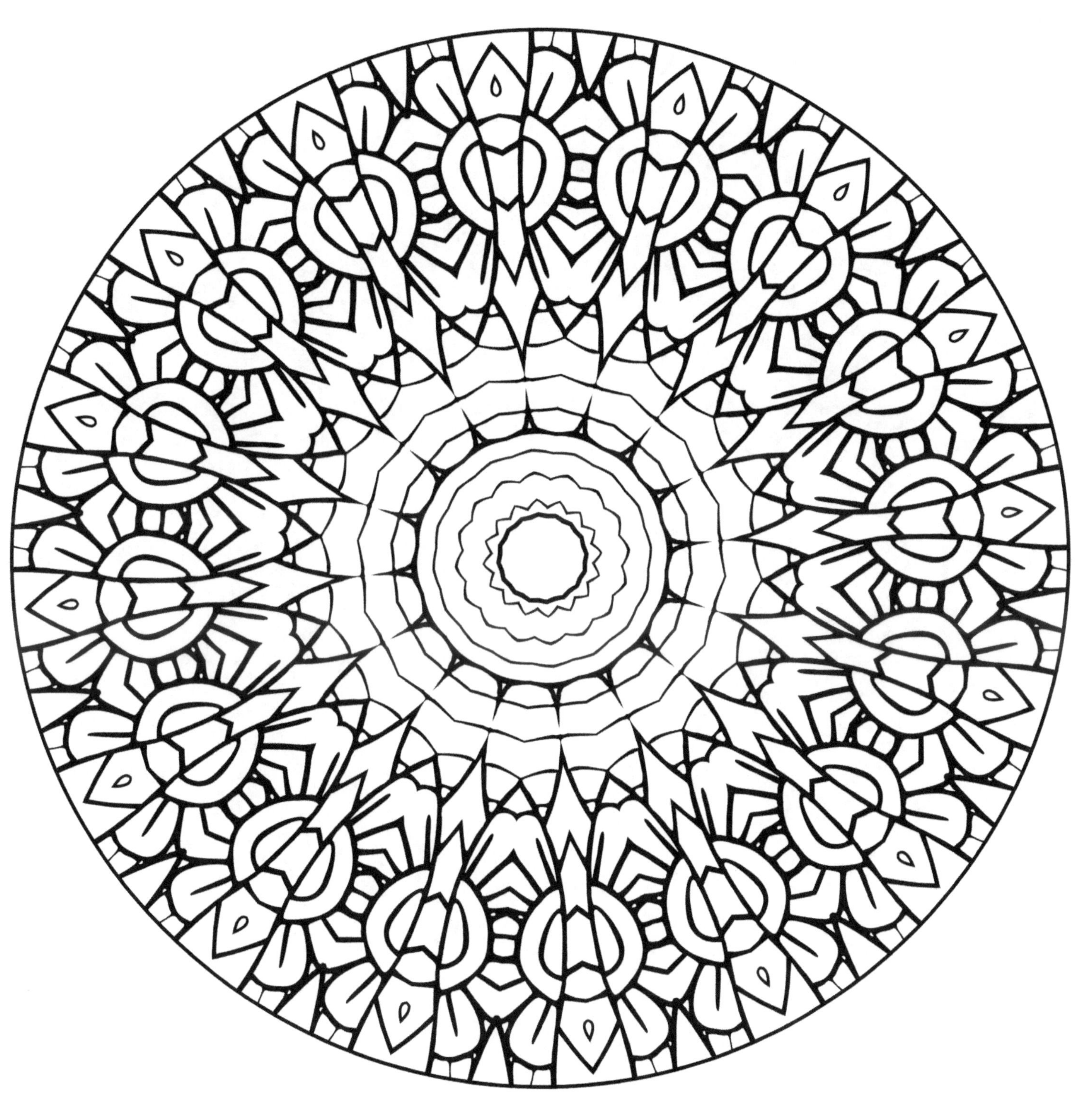

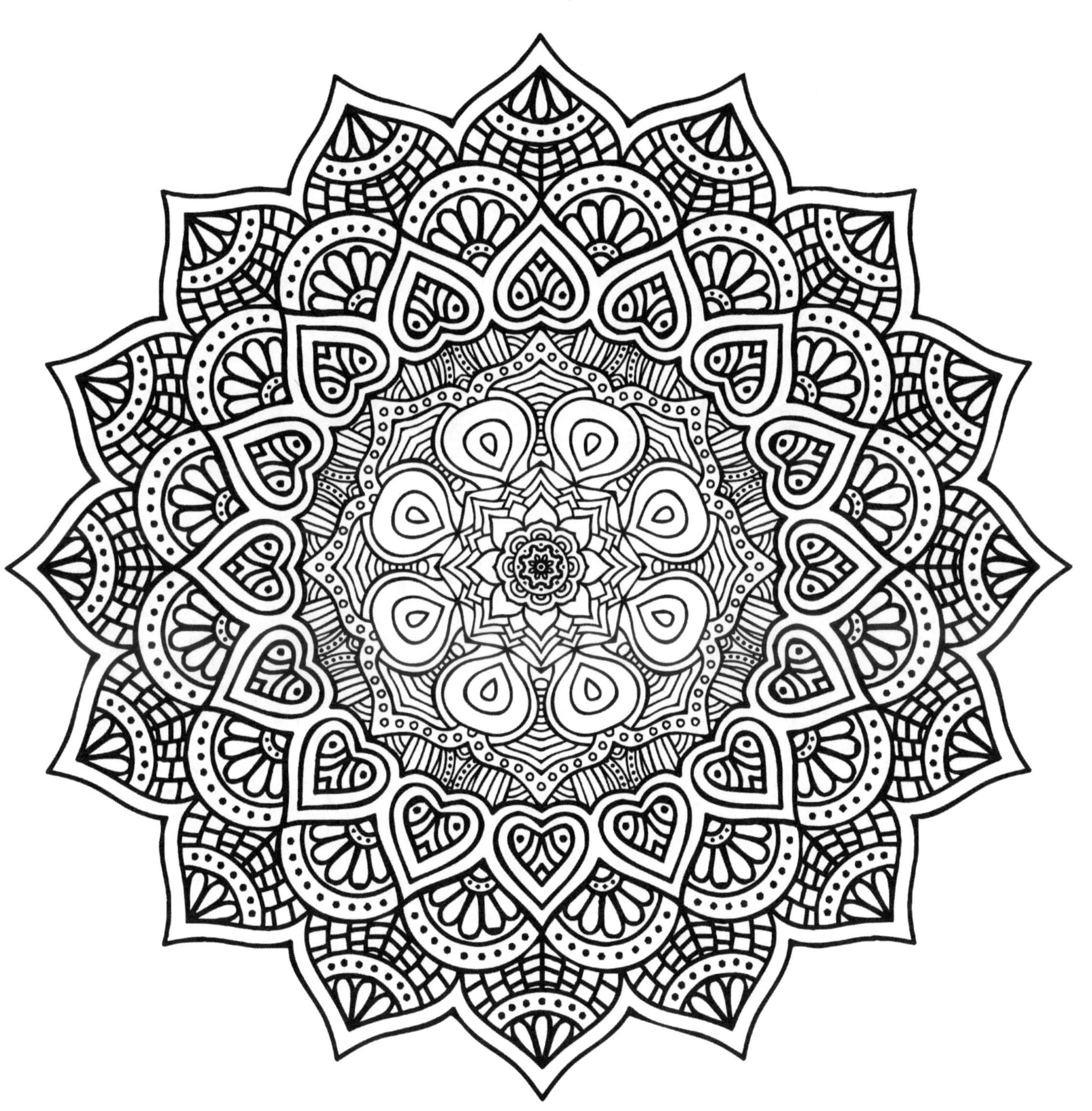

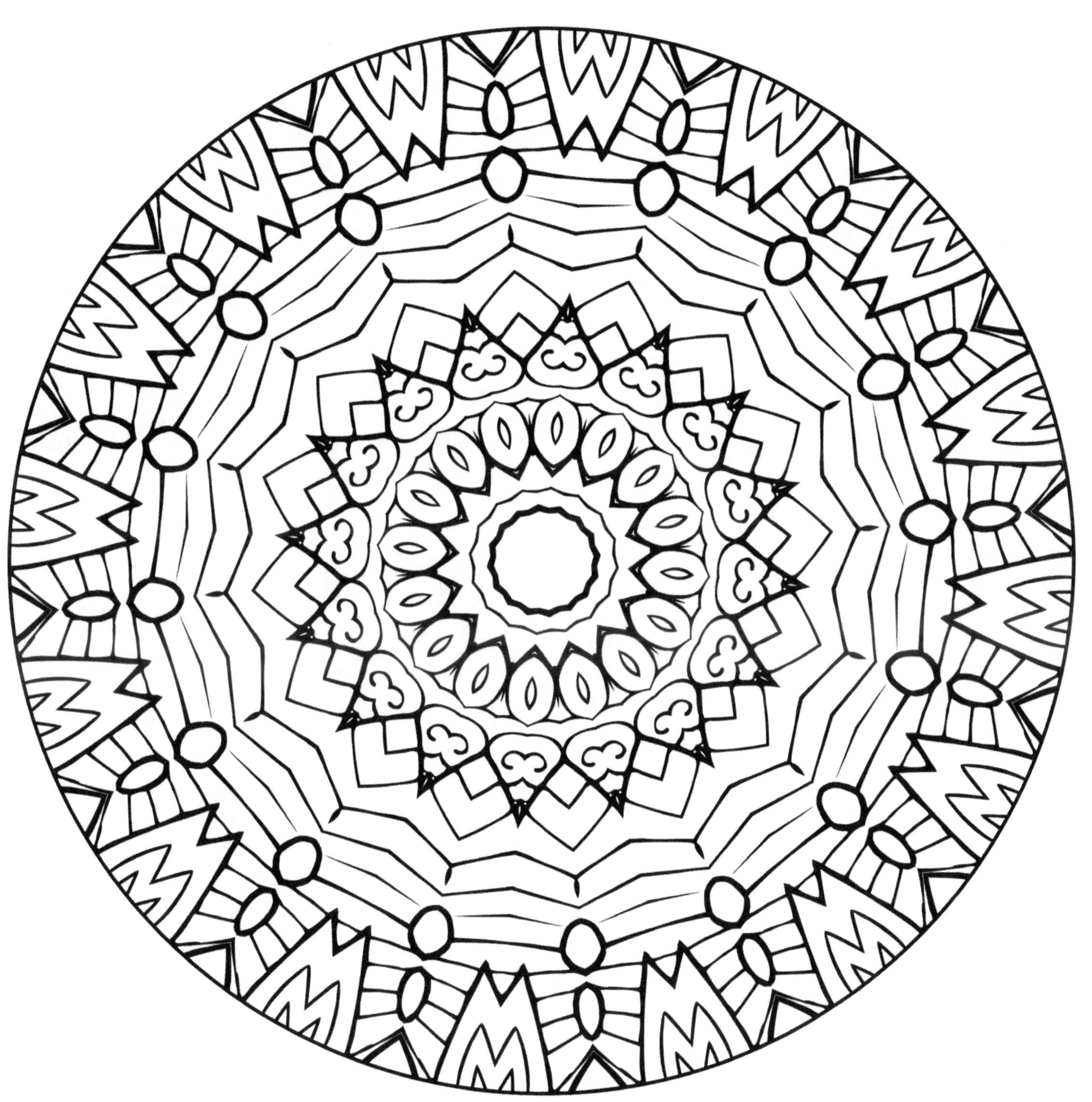

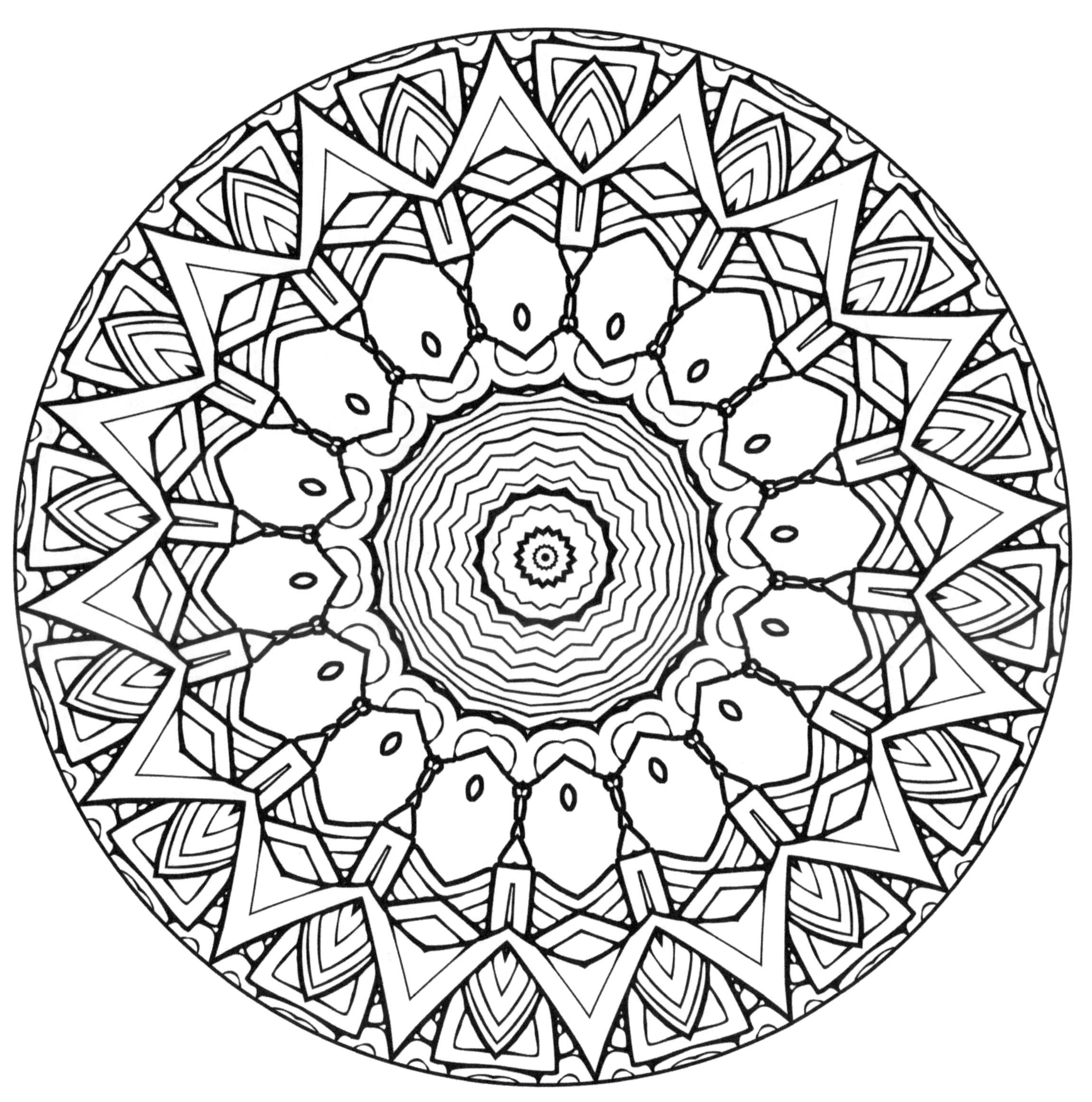

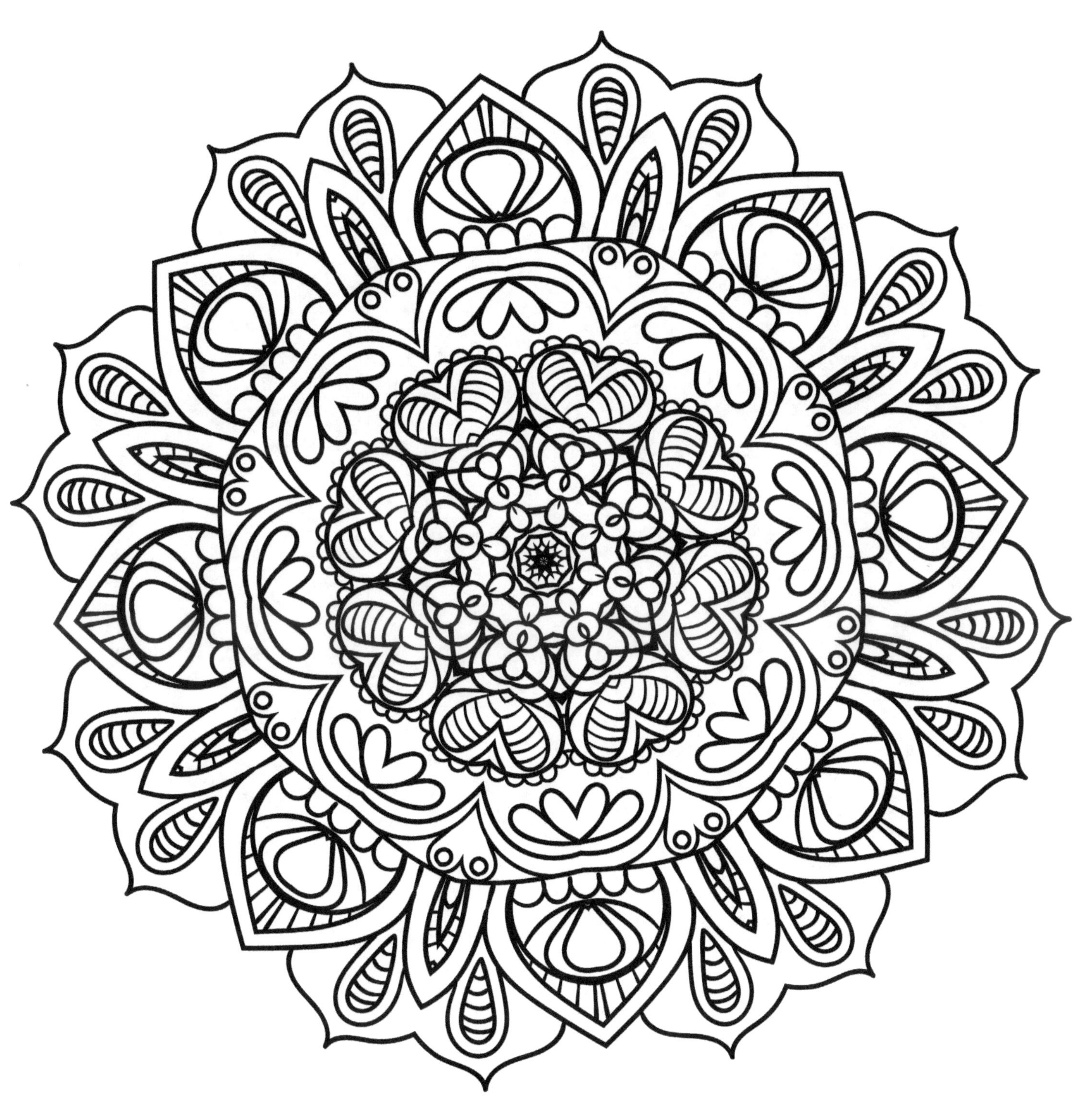

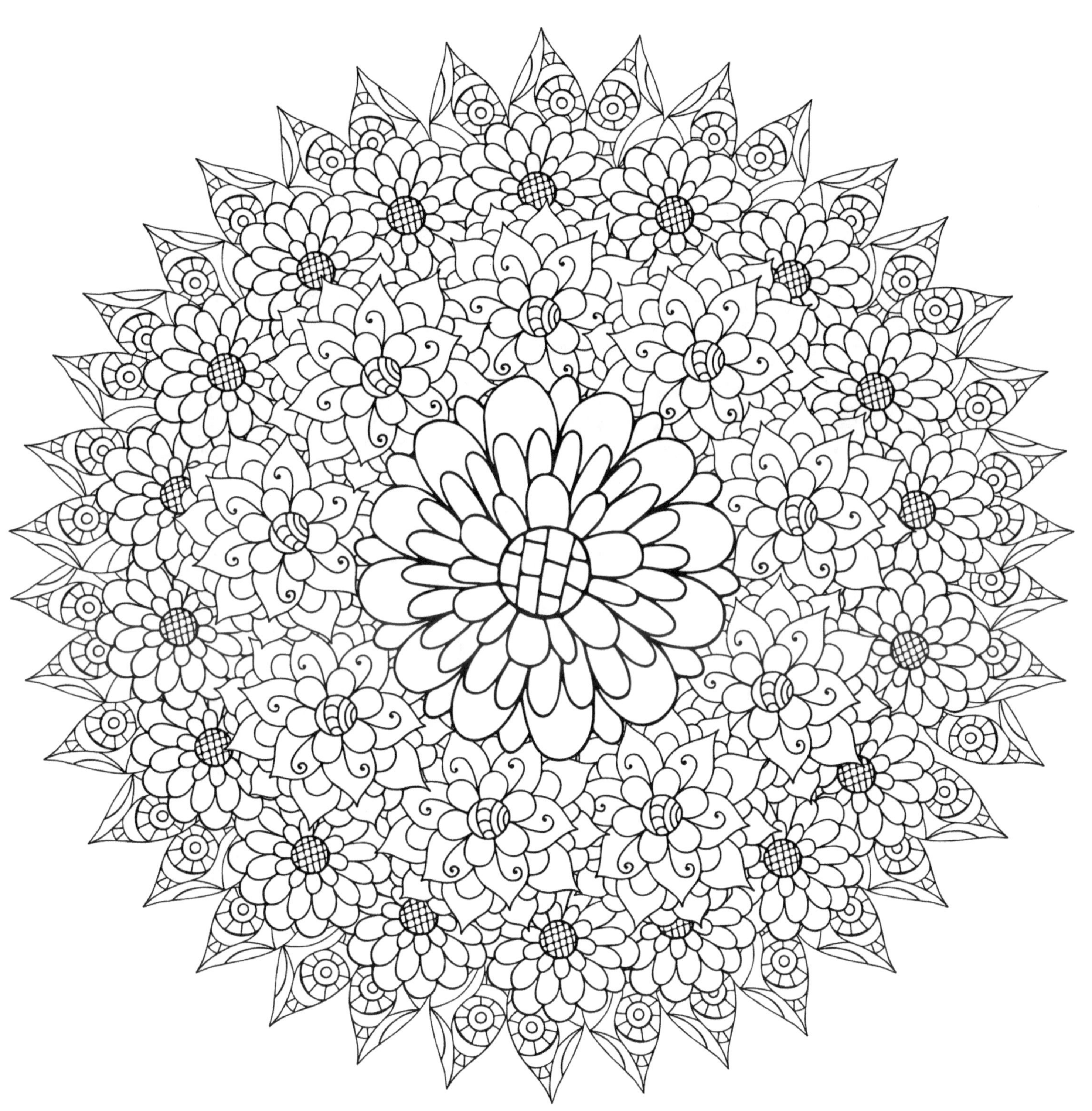

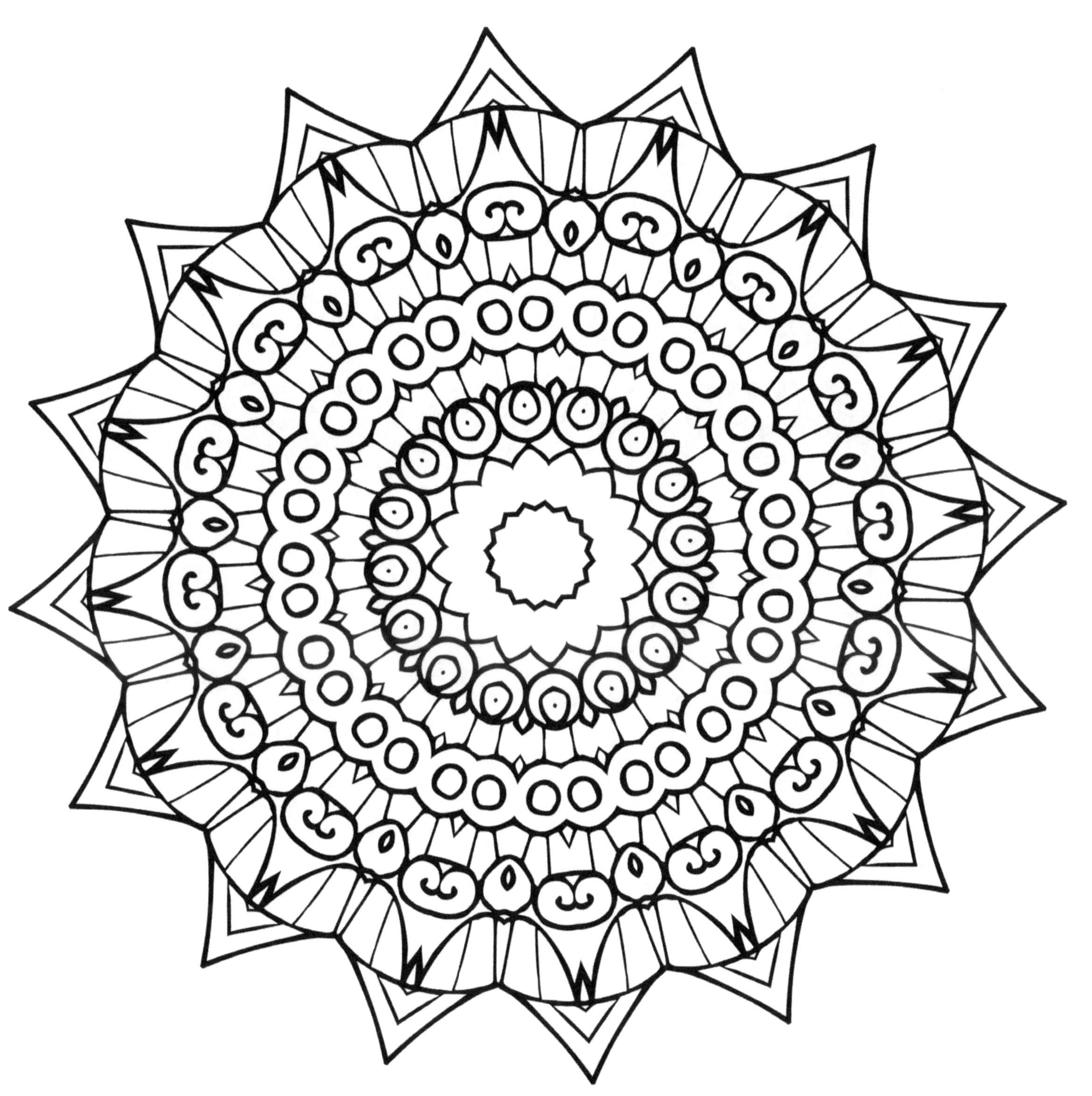

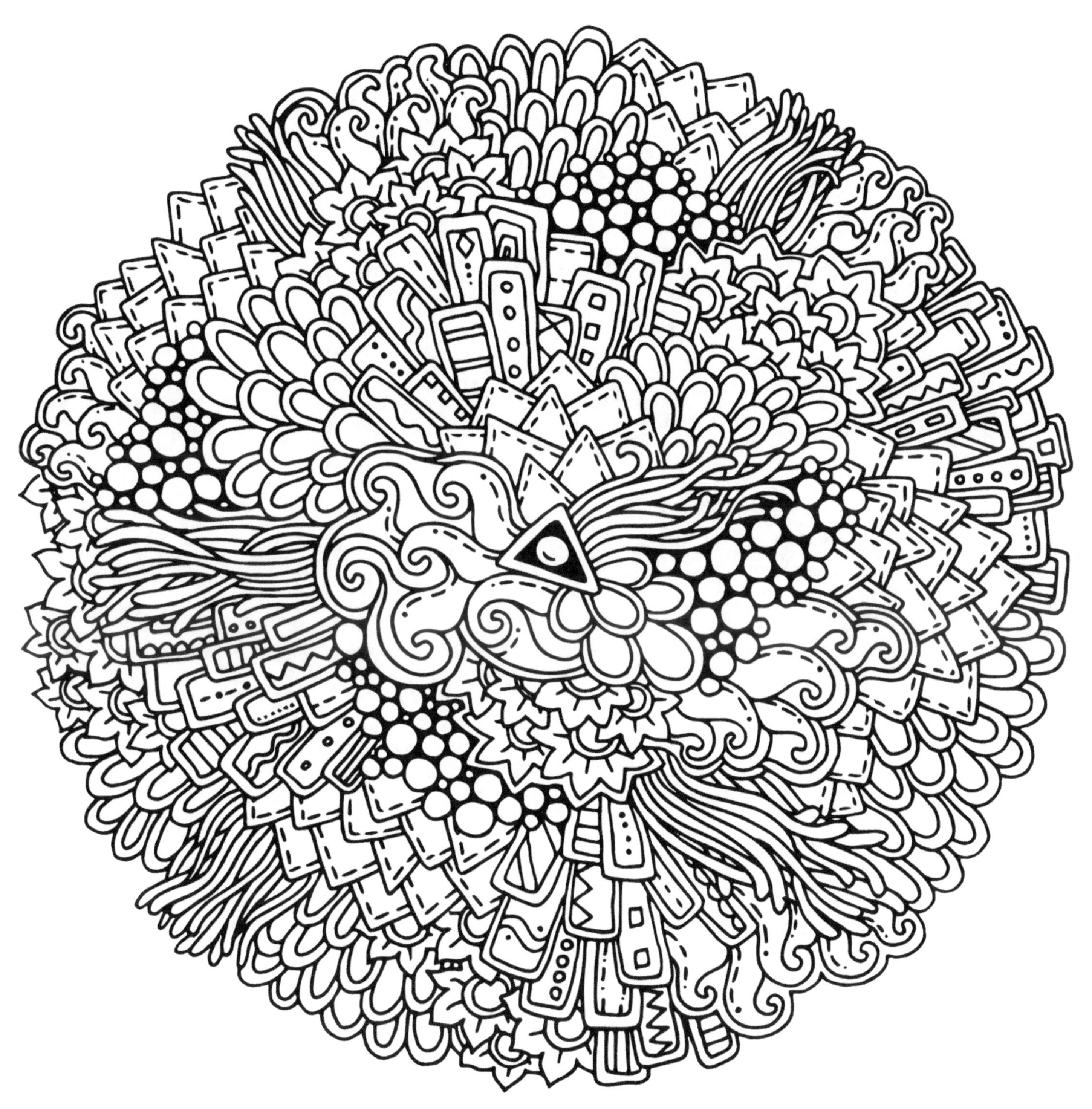

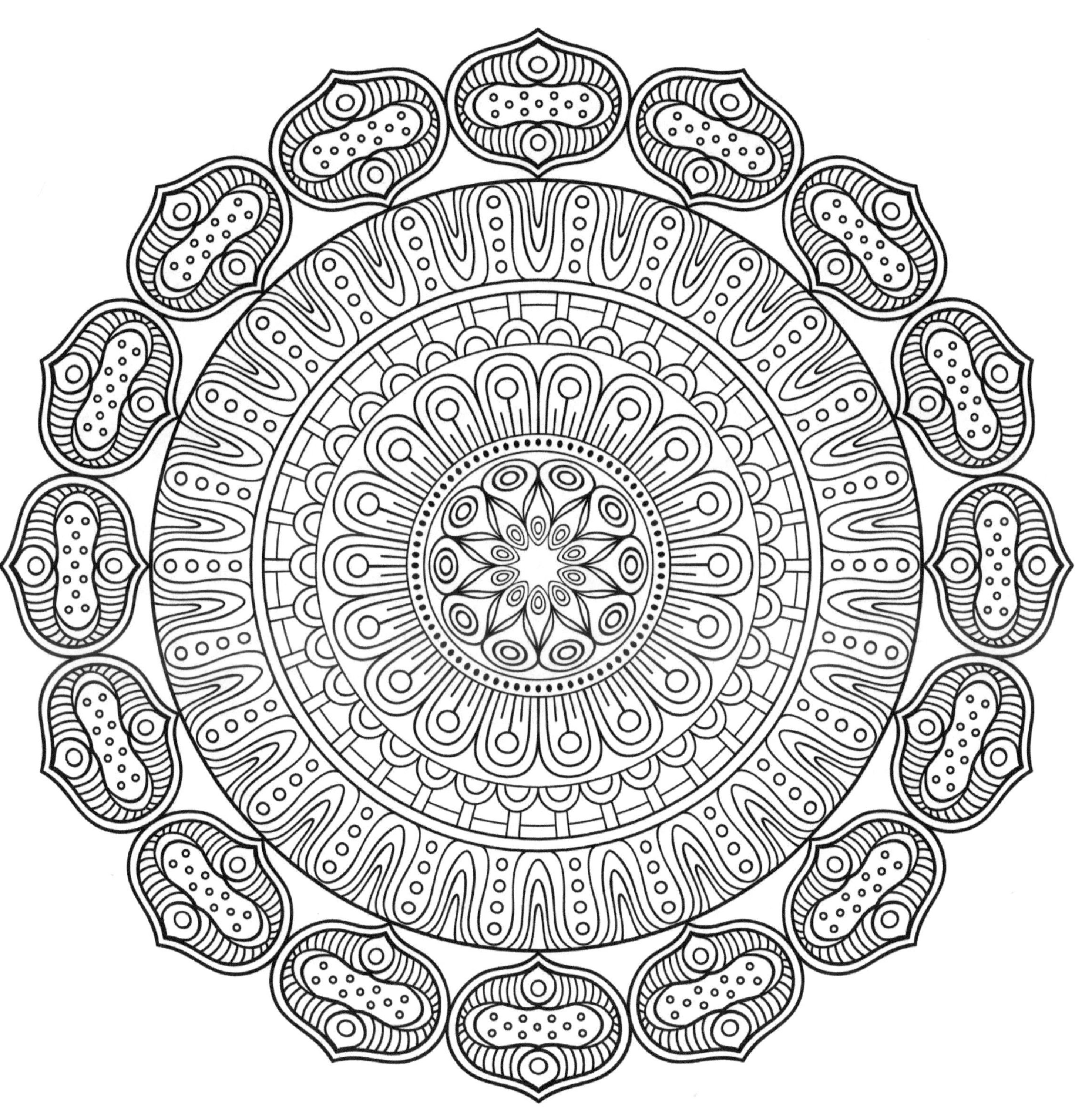

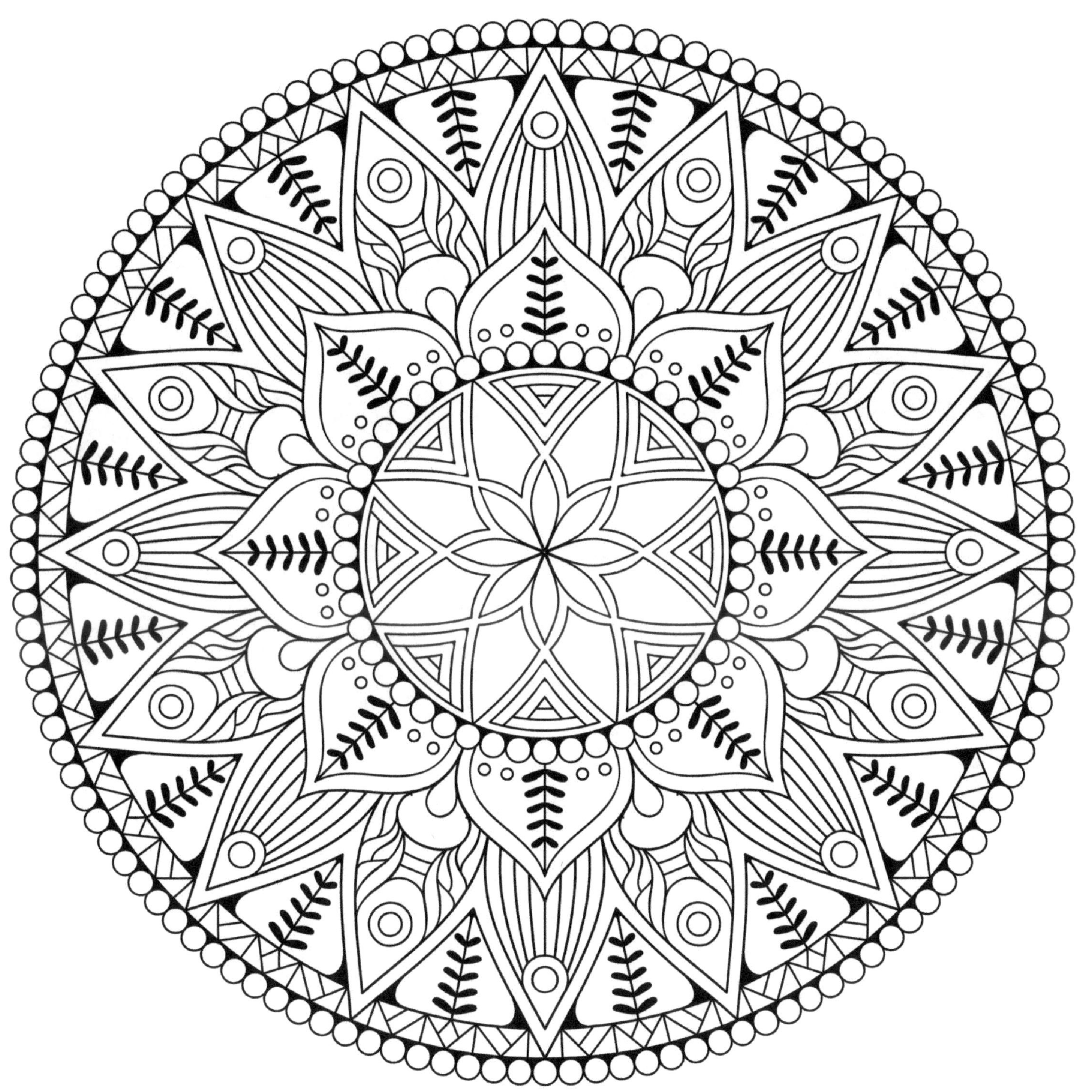

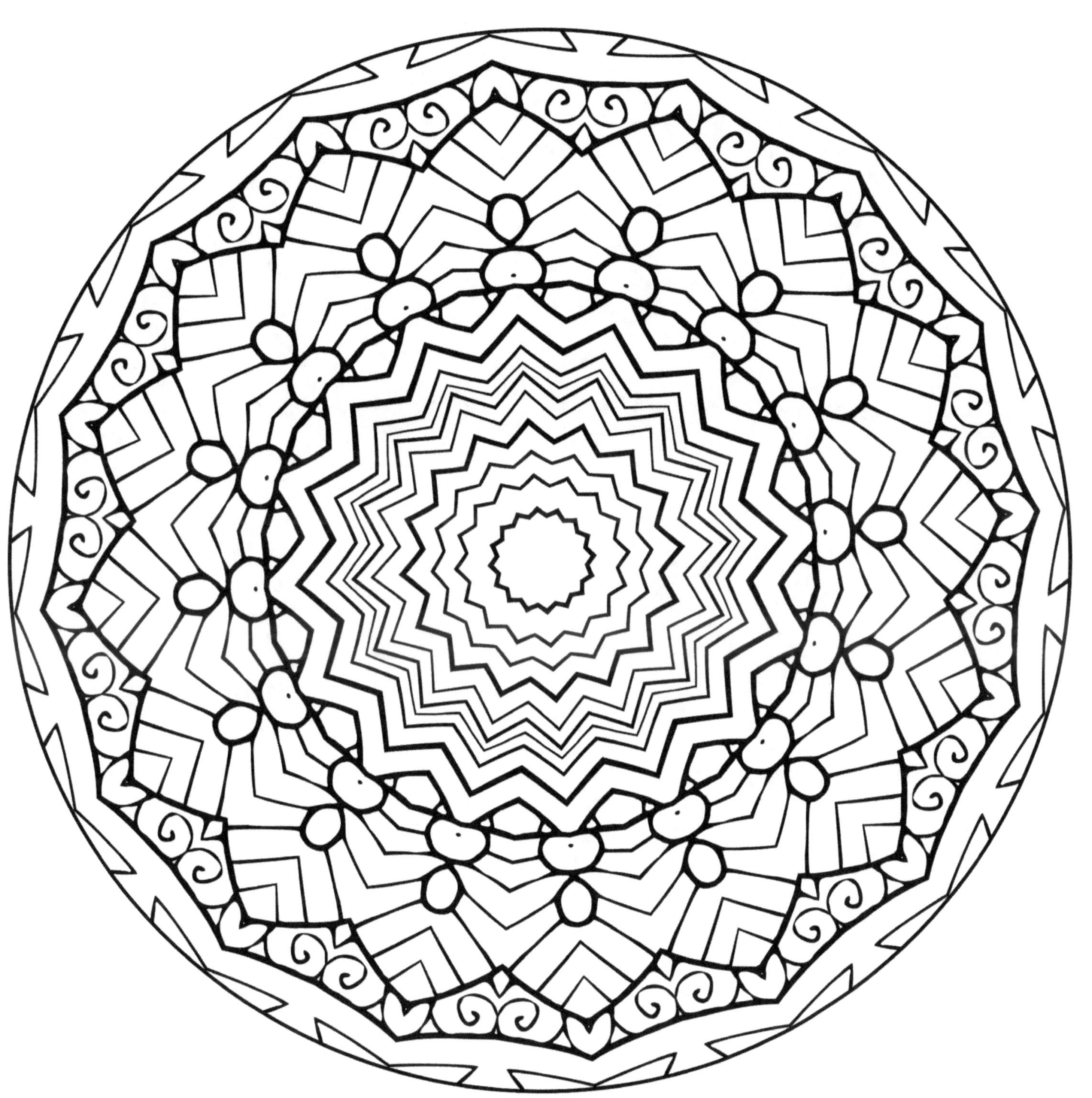

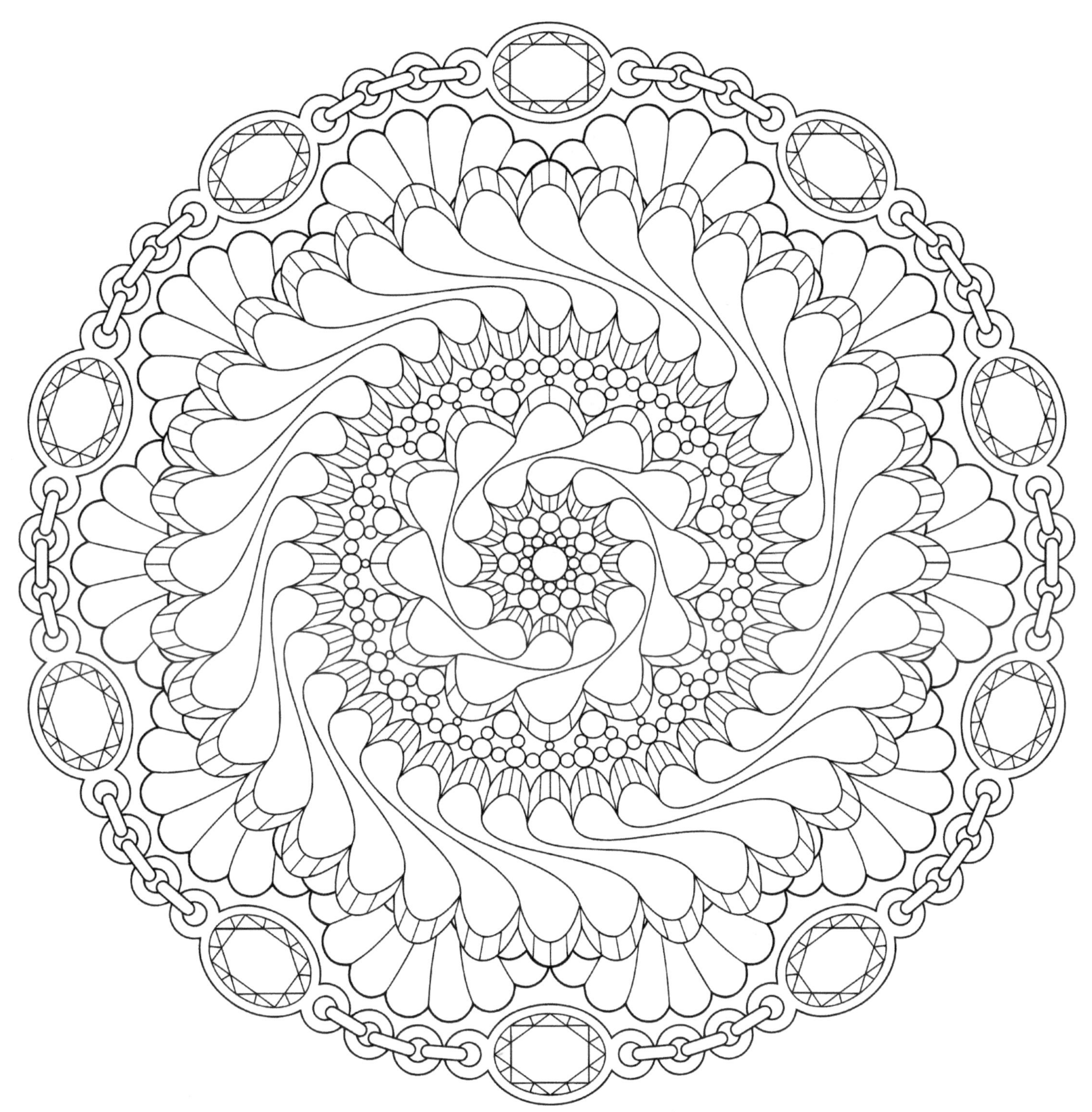

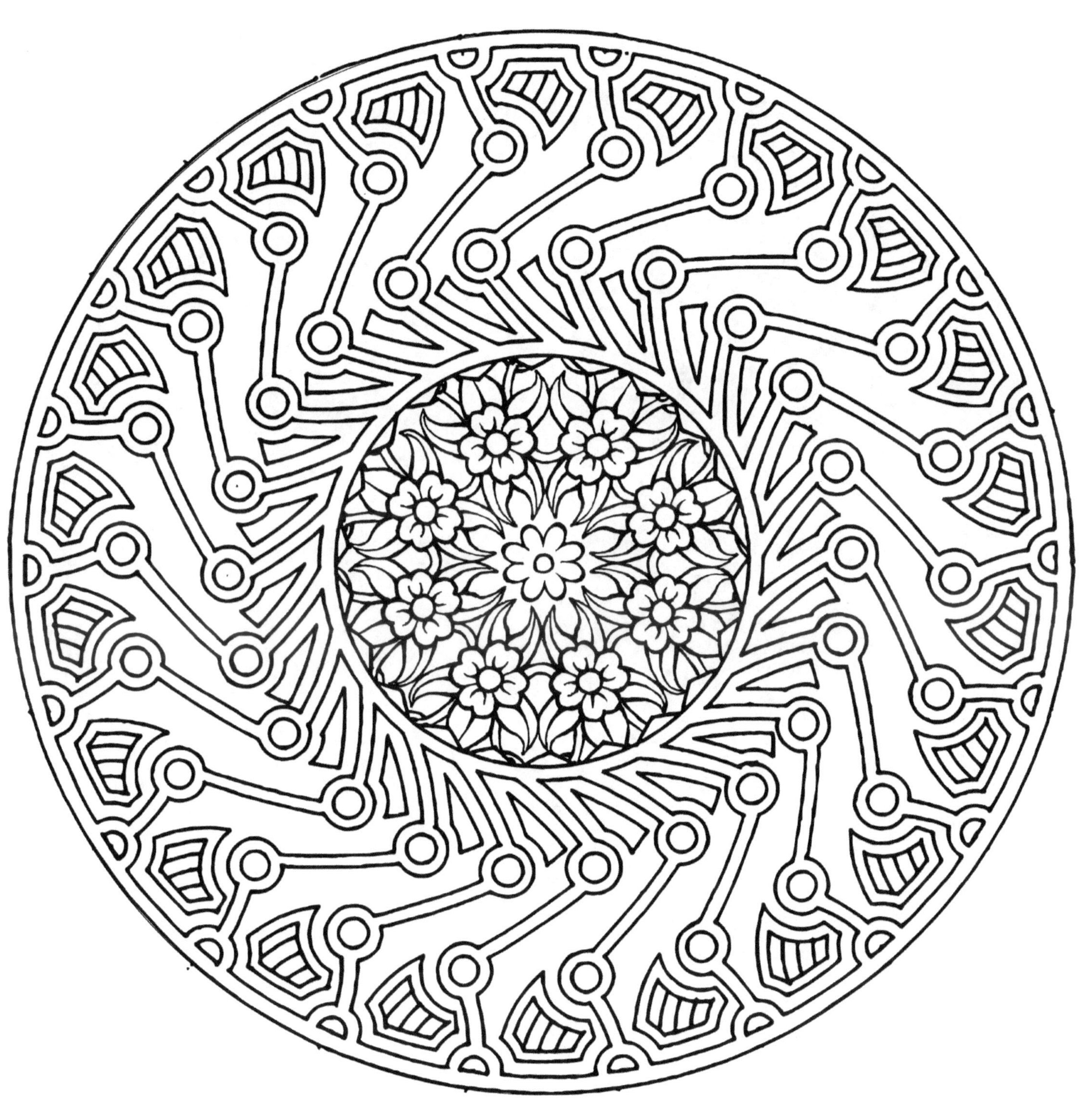

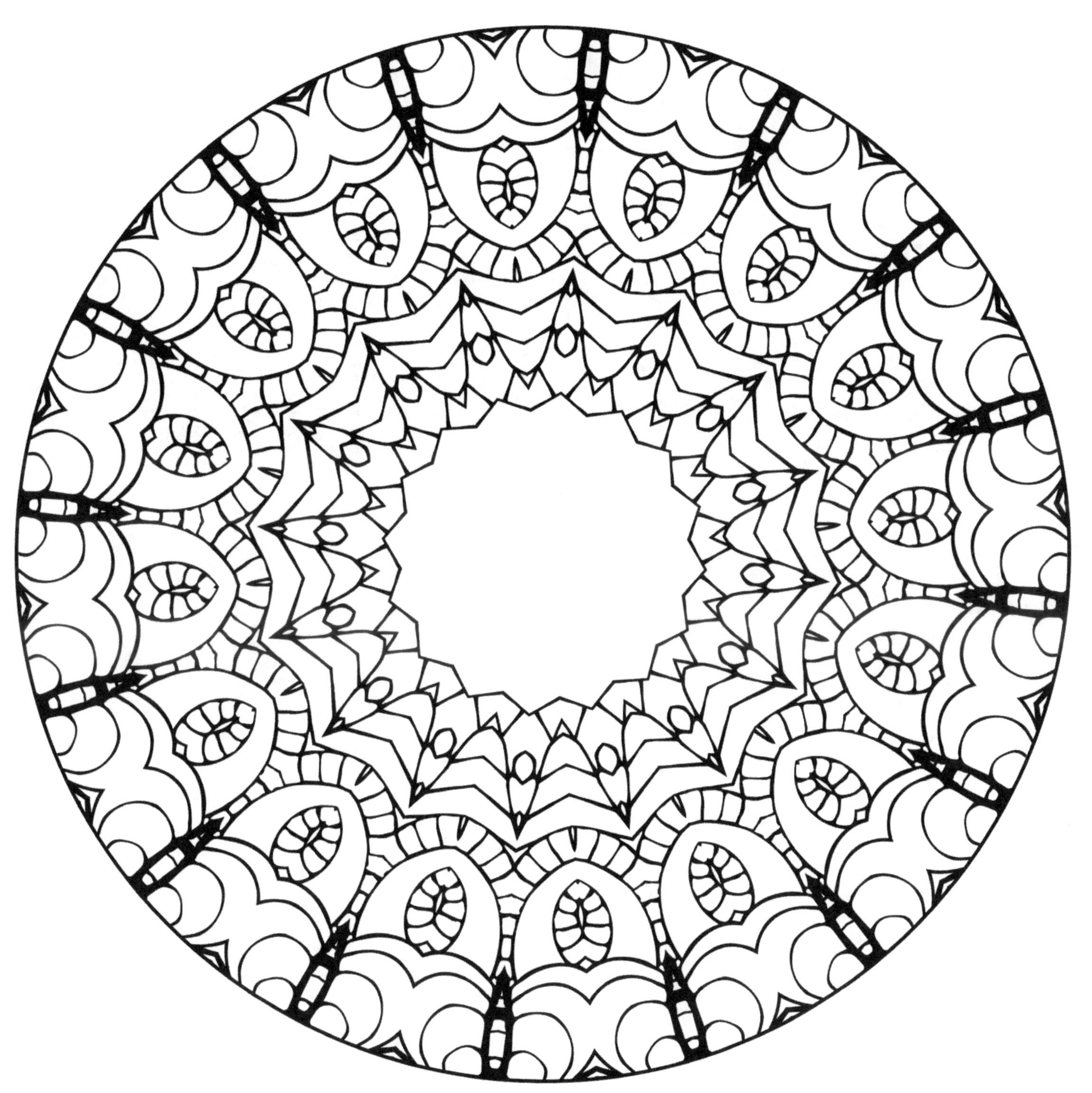

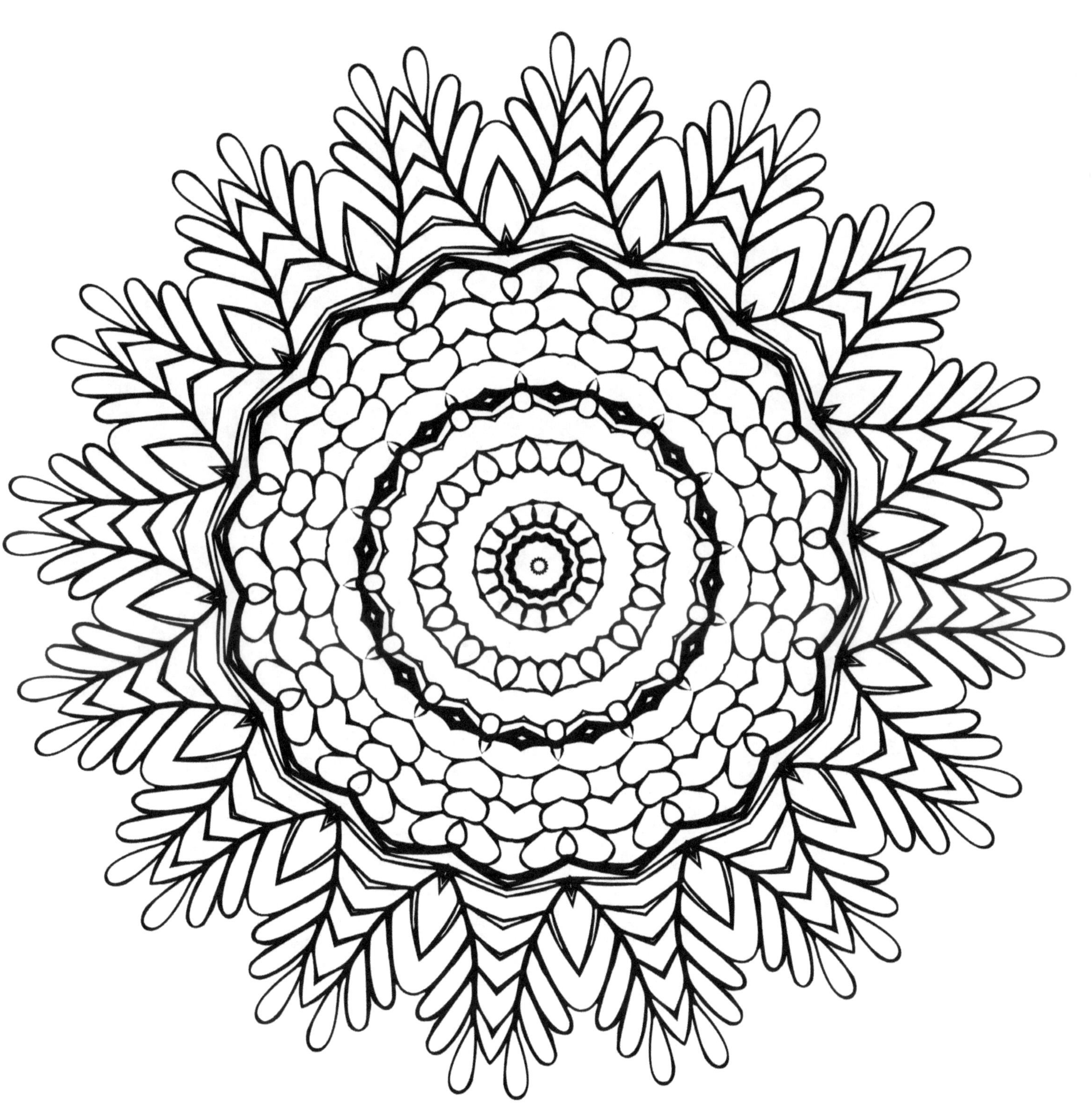

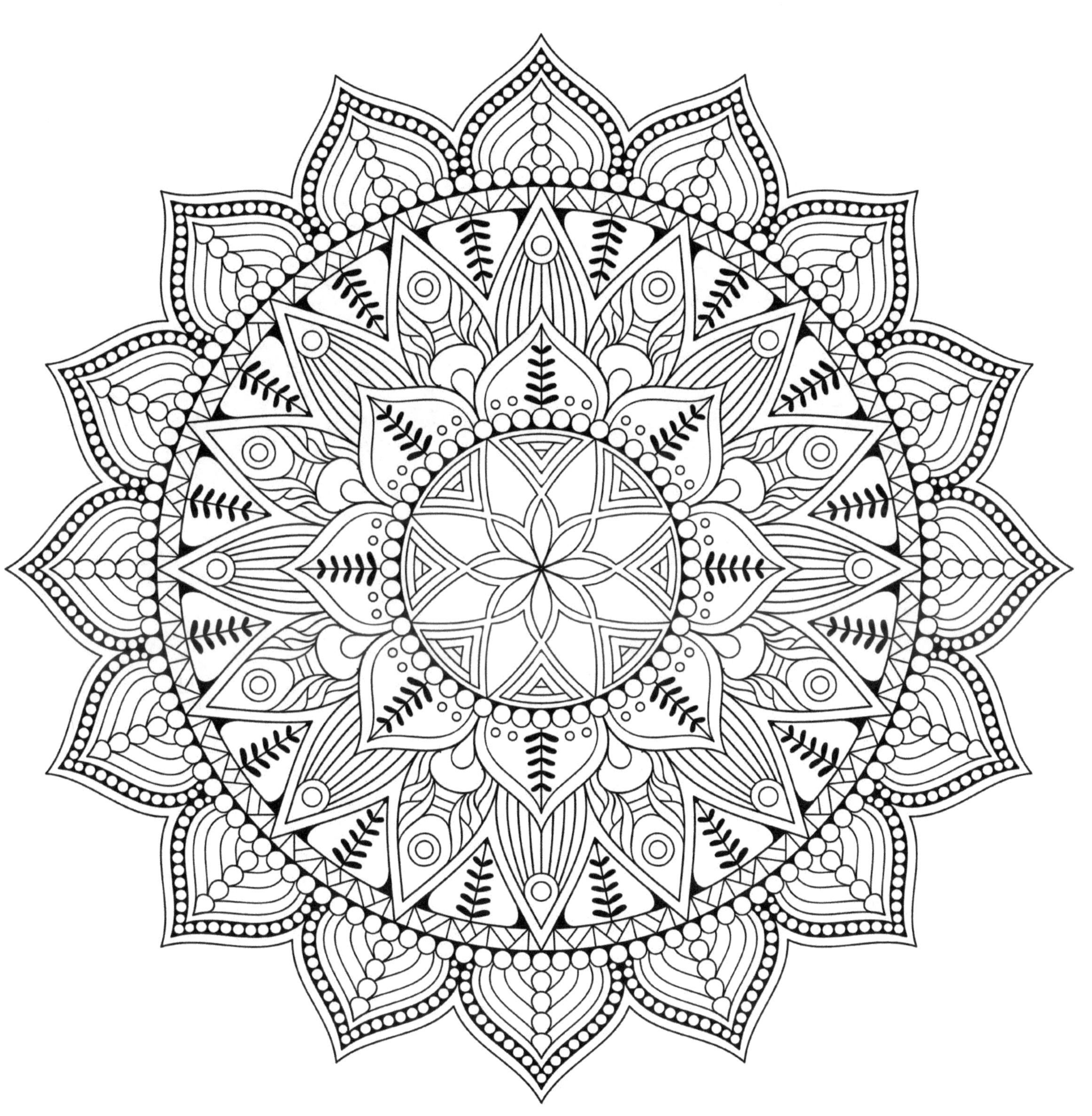

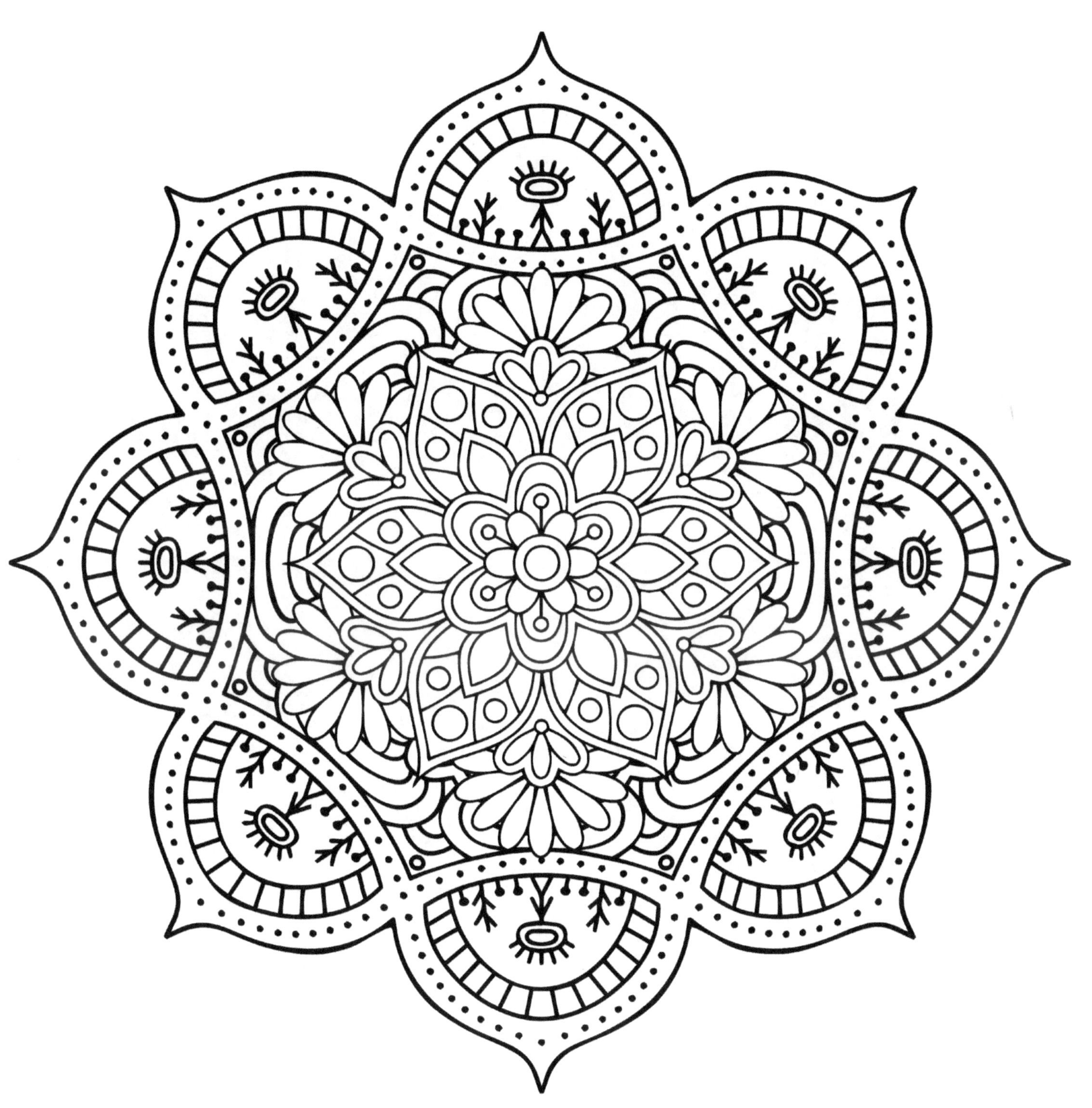

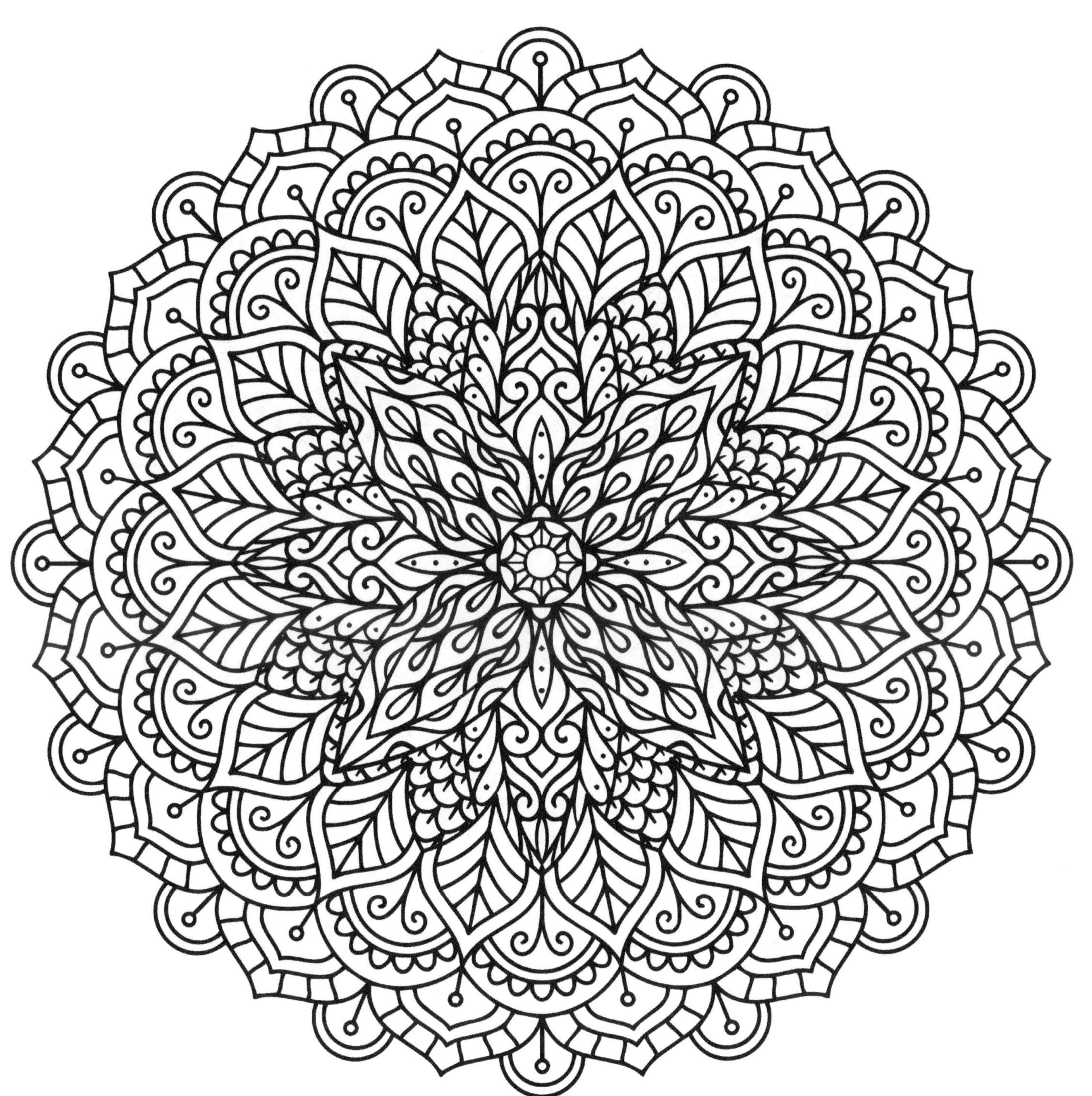

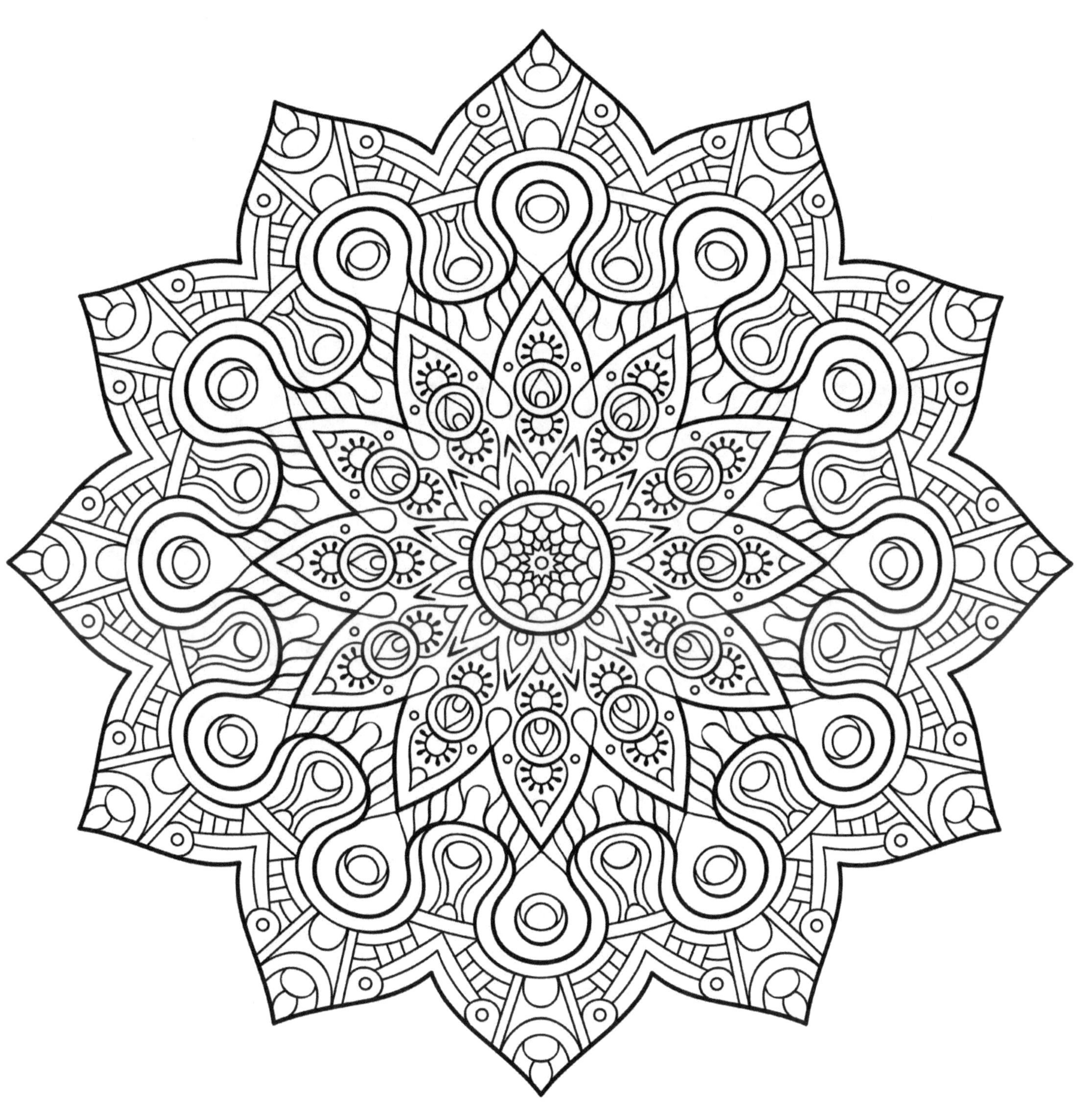

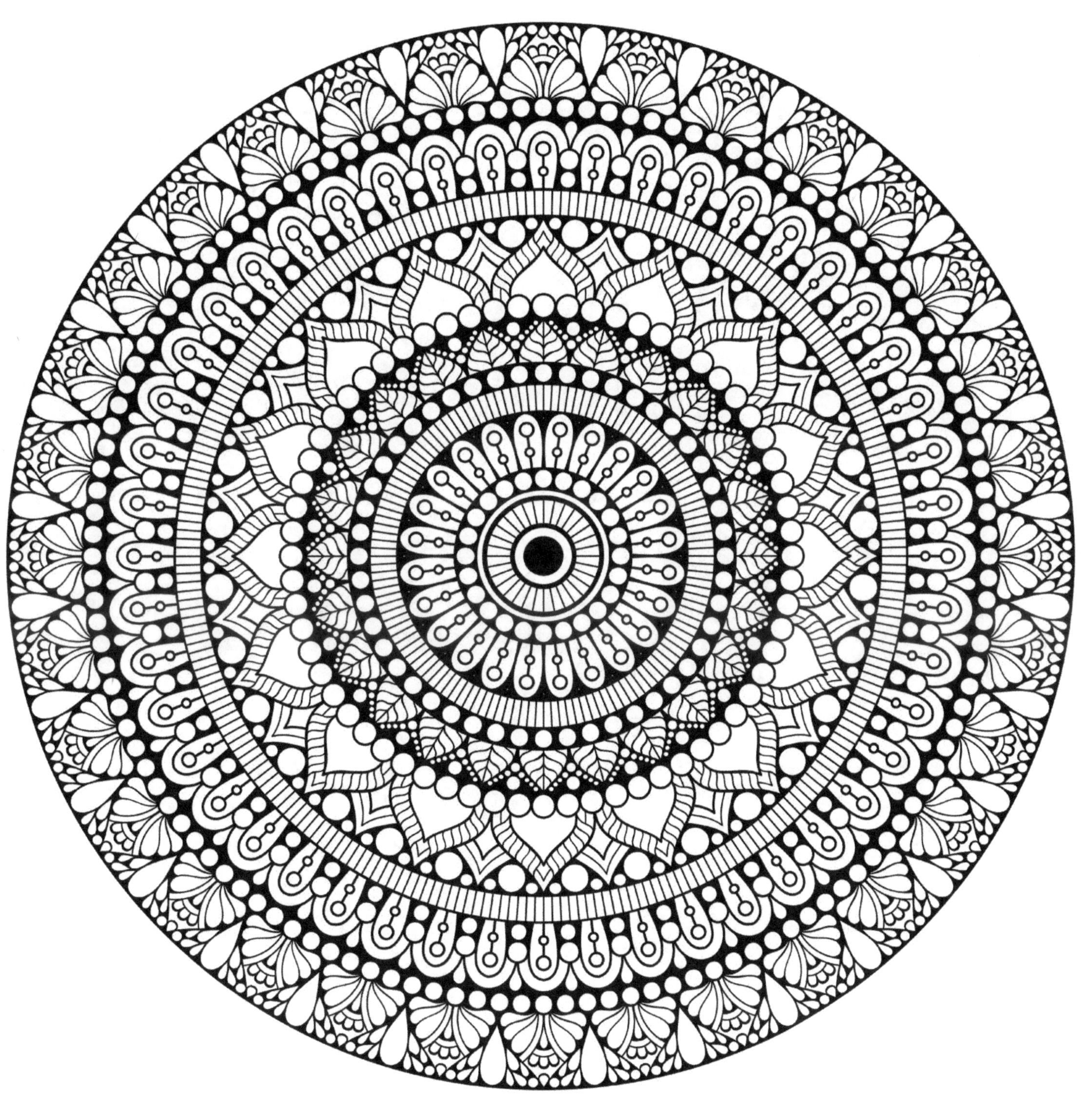

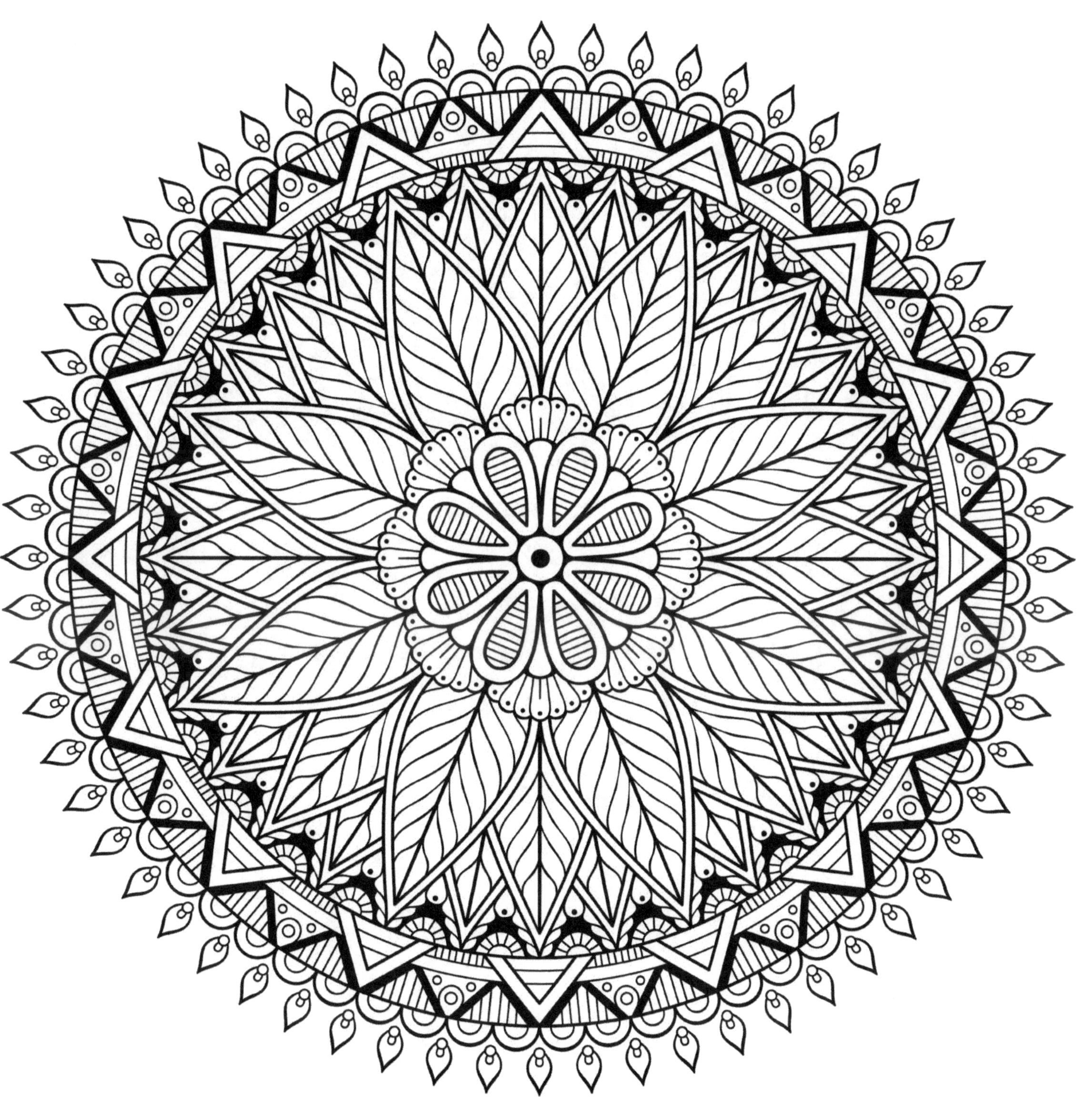

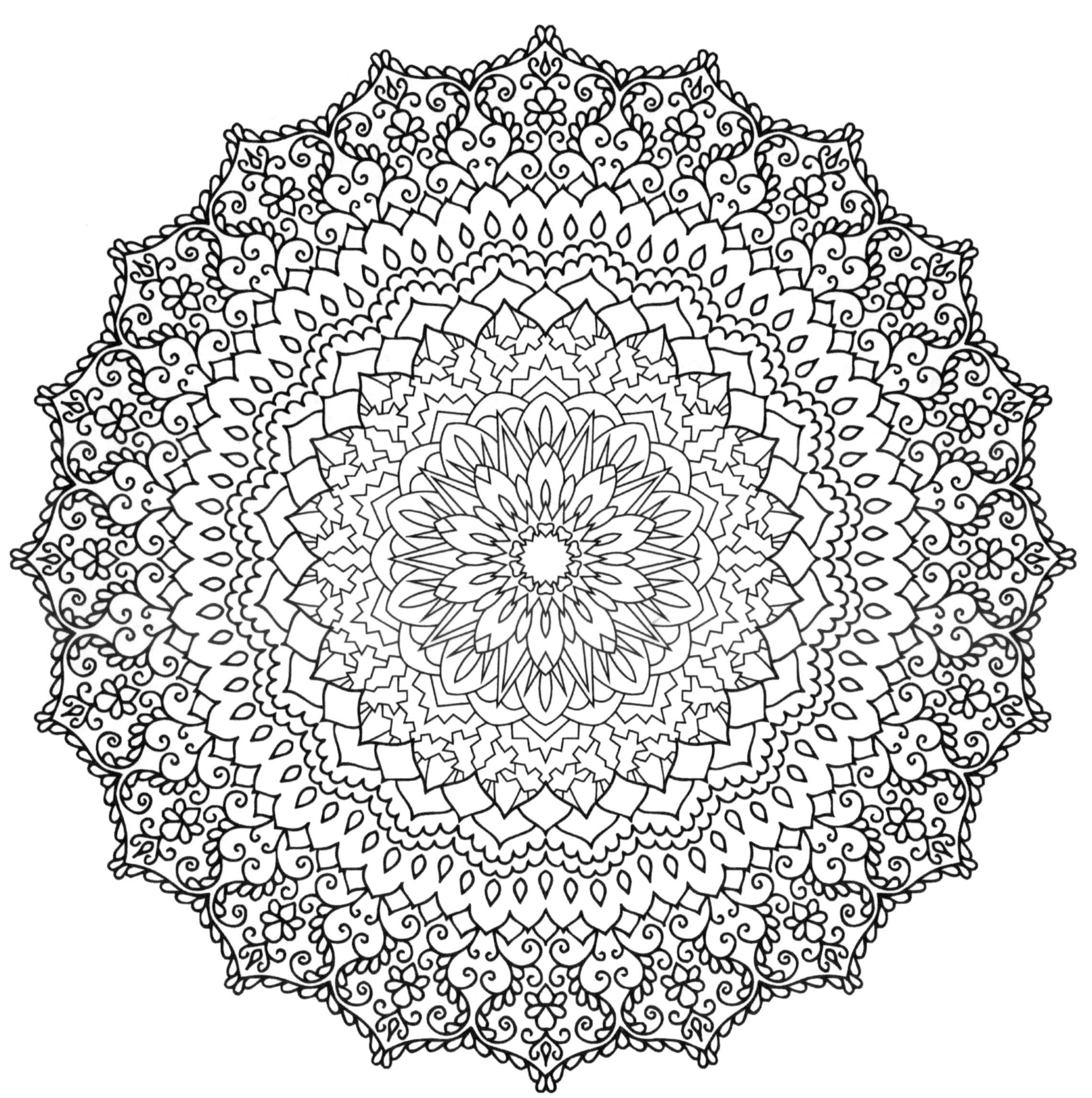

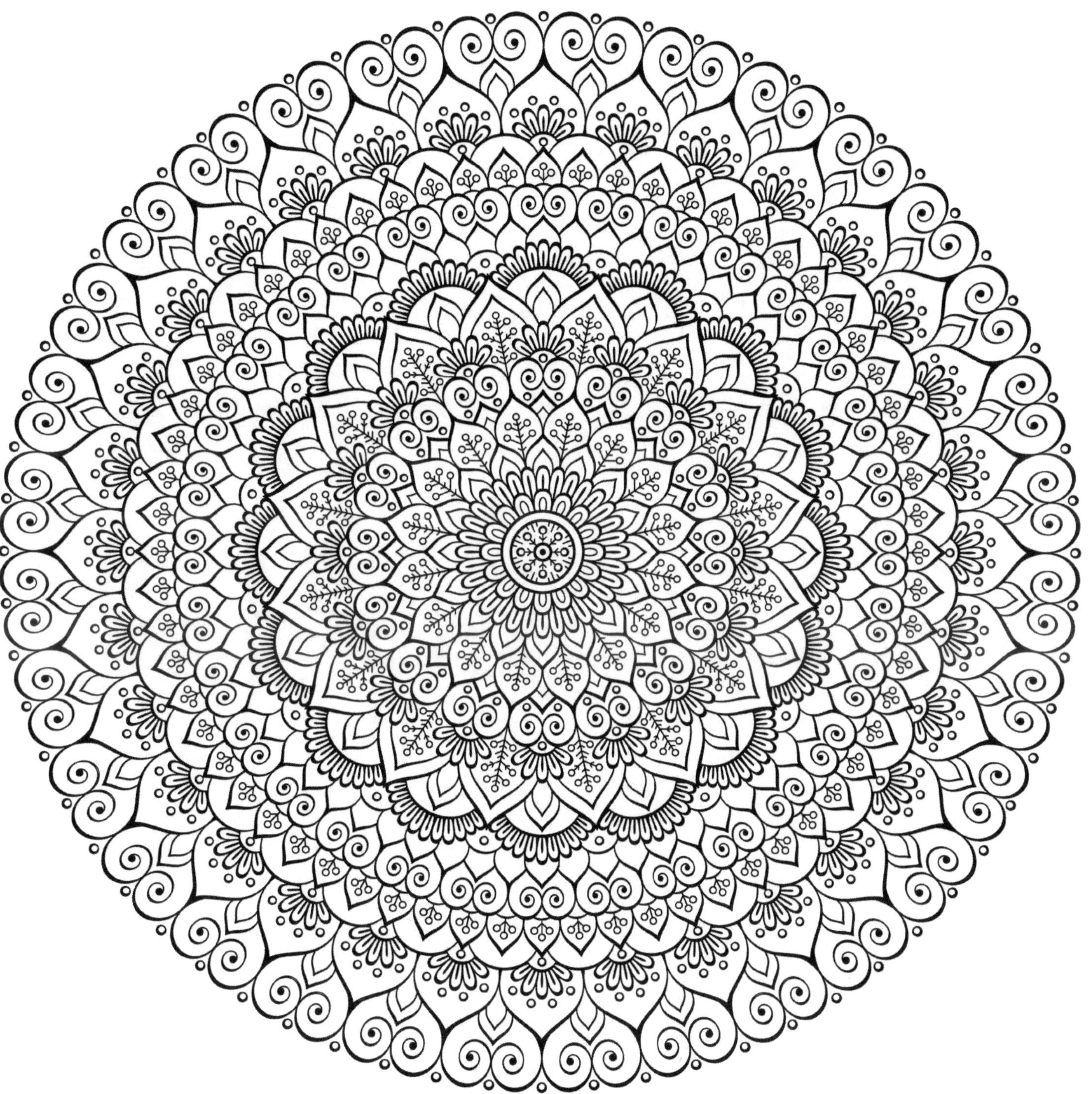

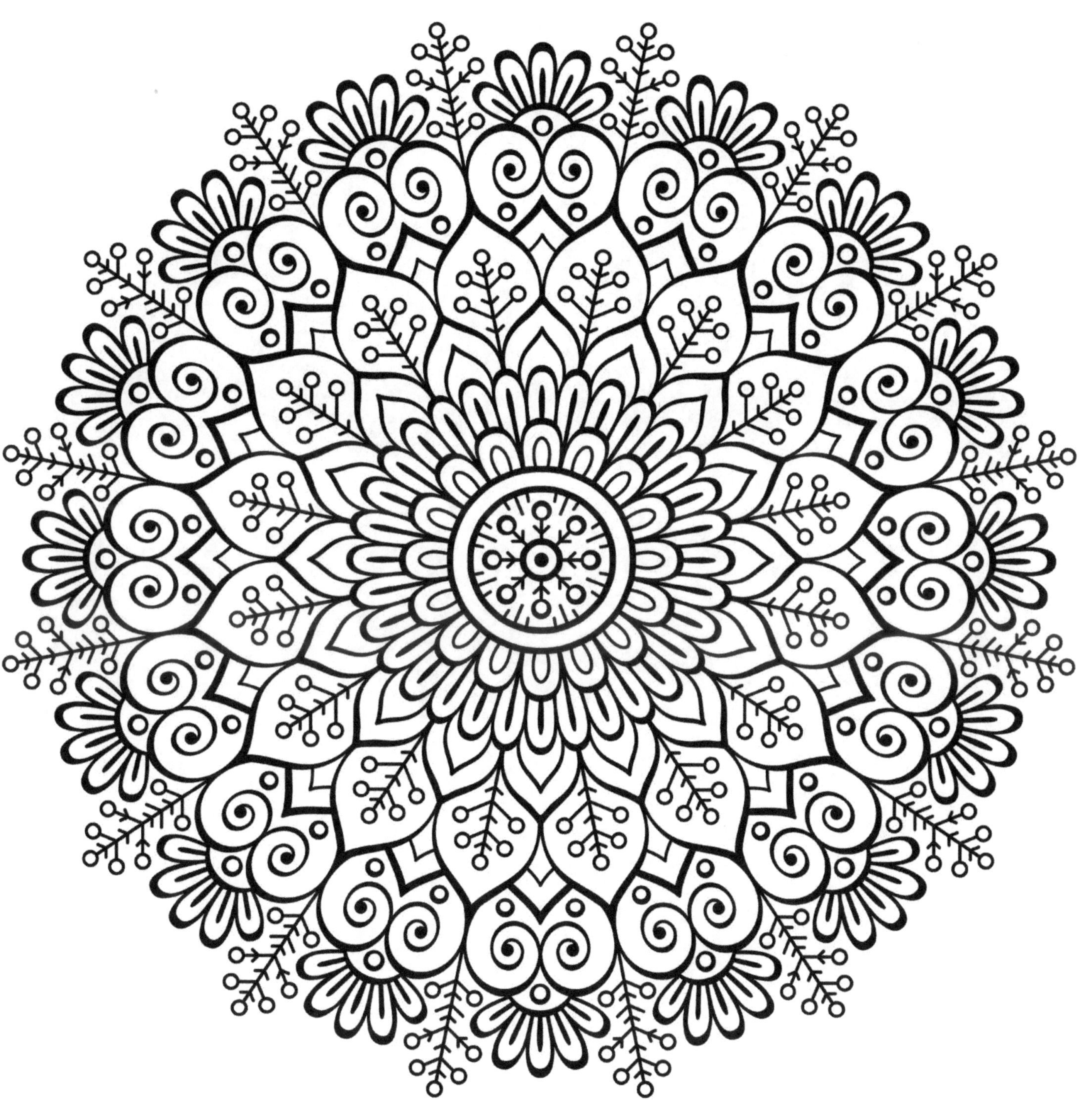

DEAR FELLOW ARTIST,

I hope that you've enjoyed the wonders of coloring the third book in our **Mellowing Mandalas** series of gorgeous, custom-drawn mandalas for stress reduction. I hope that you've had as much fun coloring in these drawings as I had in putting this book together. Please look for the other two books in the Joy Rose *Coloring With Joy* series of adult coloring books. If you have comments, or suggestions, please email me at:

COLORINGWITHJOYPUBLISHING@GMAIL.COM

I'd love to hear from you. We're always looking for your input. Your ideas, what you like to color. Was this book easy enough? Hard enough? Do you want more mandalas like page 82? Page 46? Let us know. We are creating new books and new designs constantly--for *you*. Look for new books in our **Mellowing Mandalas** series of adult coloring books, which should be in bookstores now.

COLOR WITH JOY,

Joy Rose

Page Intentionally Left Blank For Your Use

Page Intentionally Left Blank For Your Use

www.ingramcontent.com/pod-product-compliance
Lightning Source LLC
LaVergne TN
LVHW081419110826
845149LV00010B/1795

9780997813340